Engaging Technology in Theological Education

D0870799

THE COMMUNICATION, CULTURE, AND RELIGION SERIES
SERIES EDITORS: PAUL SOUKUP, S.J., AND FRANCES FORDE PLUDE

The **Communication, Culture, and Religion** Series publishes books that explore the religious and theological implications of contemporary and popular culture, especially as manifest in mass or interactive media and media products. The series encourages a dialogue in which communication practices and products shed light on religion and, in turn, religious reflection deepens an understanding of communication studies.

Engaging Technology in Theological Education: All That We Can't Leave Behind
by Mary E. Hess

Seeking Goodness and Beauty: The Use of the Arts in Theological Ethics
Edited by Patricia Lamoureux and Kevin O'Neil, C.Ss.R

Nourishing Faith Through Fiction: Reflections of the Apostles' Creed in Literature and Film
By John R. May

From One Medium to Another: Communicating the Bible through Multimedia
Edited by Robert Hodgson and Paul Soukup, S.J.

New Image of Religious Film
By John R. May

Imaging the Divine: Jesus and Christ-Figures in Film
By Lloyd Baugh, S.J.

Engaging Technology in Theological Education

All That We Can't Leave Behind

Mary E. Hess

ROWMAN & LITTLEFIELD PUBLISHERS, INC.
Lanham • Boulder • New York • Toronto • Oxford

ROWMAN & LITTLEFIELD PUBLISHERS, INC.

Published in the United States of America
by Rowman & Littlefield Publishers, Inc.
A wholly owned subsidiary of The Rowman & Littlefield Publishing Group, Inc.
4501 Forbes Boulevard, Suite 200, Lanham, Maryland 20706
www.rowmanlittlefield.com

PO Box 317
Oxford
OX2 9RU, UK

British Library Cataloguing in Publication Information Available

Library of Congress Cataloging-in-Publication Data

Hess, Mary E.
  Engaging technology in theological education : all that we can't leave behind /
Mary E. Hess.
     p. cm. — (The communication, culture, and religion series)
  Includes bibliographical references and index.
  ISBN 0-7425-3223-2 (cloth : alk. paper) — ISBN 0-7425-3224-0 (pbk. : alk. paper)
  1. Theology—Study and teaching.   2. Educational technology.   I. Title.
II. Series: Communication, culture & theology.

  BV4020.H47 2005
  230'.078ædc22   2004029353

Printed in the United States of America

⊗™ The paper used in this publication meets the minimum requirements of American
National Standard for Information Sciences—Permanence of Paper for Printed Library
Materials, ANSI/NISO Z39.48-1992.

Contents

Acknowledgments

This book has its roots in watching my mother teach. She is a gifted educator working in multiple contexts—as choir director, as piano and organ teacher, as elementary school music teacher, as teacher in a university music education program. Growing up around her I learned that teaching is all about *learning* and that learning is about being open to the people and contexts around you. Such openness demands respect for the integrity of learners, regardless of whether what they want to learn is what you want to teach! Indeed, often I have learned far more from students' resistance than from ready acceptance.

The faculties with whom I have worked over the years have brought much resistance to the table as they have struggled with the role of digital technology in theological education. That resistance was a gift, pushing me to articulate the opportunities and benefits of such integration, even while it forced me to recognize the dilemmas such technologies pose. Any aid that this book might bring to the conversation can be traced to their questions, any obstacle to my own limitations.

My thanks to Jeremy Langford and Paul Soukup for believing that this book could meet a need and for helping me to see it through the process from idea to completion.

I need to thank, in particular, certain of my colleagues who have consistently listened patiently to my passionate diatribes about media culture and theological education and challenged me to make a difference. They have provided a wonderfully fruitful learning medium for my own growth: A. K. M. Adams, Richard Ascough, Rebekah Bane, Trevor Bechtel, Jim Caccamo, Scott Cormode, Mary Hinkle, Lucinda Huffaker, Todd Johnson, Vic Klimoski, Alice Loddigs, Adán Medrano, Paul Myhre, Richard Nysse, Dianne Oliver, Jim Rafferty, Jan Viktora, and Hal Weldin.

Finally, I need to thank the people who most persistently challenge and inform my learning: my partner, Eric, and our children, Alex and Nathaniel. Eric's creativity and imagination, along with his commitment to technology used in appropriate ways, sustains me in this quest. His full partnership in maintaining a home and raising our children has freed me to work on projects like this book. Alex, though only twelve as of this writing, has already gone far beyond me in his work with digital projects. His energy, intense curiosity, and eager engagement with all things digital reminds me that soon there will be no question that digital technologies should be integrated into theological education—our students will do it for us, and perhaps in spite of us. And Nathaniel, the youngest in our home, soaks up learning like a huge natural sponge. His laughter and generous hugs remind me that God is always among us, delighting in children.

The publisher and author are grateful for permission to reprint the following: Portions of chapter 1 appear as "Rescripting Christian Education for Performative Practice," in *Belief in Media: Cultural Perspectives on Media and Christianity,* edited by Mary Hess, Peter Horsfield, and Adán Medrano (Aldershot: Ashgate, 2005). Portions of chapter 3 appear as "Rich Treasure in Jars of Clay" in *The Conviction of Things Not Seen: Worship and Ministry in the 21st Century,* edited by Todd Johnson, (Grand Rapids, MI: Brazos Press, 2002). Portions of chapter 5 appear as "Pedagogy and Theology in Cyberspace: All That We Can't Leave Behind," published in *Teaching Theology and Religion* 5, no. 1 (February 2002). Portions of chapter 6 appear as "White Religious Educators and Unlearning Racism: Can We Find a Way?" in the journal *Religious Education* 93, no. 1, (winter 1998). Portions of chapter 7 were first presented at the American Theological Library Association's 2003 annual meeting and subsequently published in the association's proceedings.

Introduction

This book grew out of several years of working with dedicated teachers at a variety of graduate theological schools. Each school is different, each one has specific issues unique to its context, but in each setting similar questions arose, similar fears were voiced, and similar energy grew as we identified promising new opportunities. In the beginning of this journey I was a freshly minted PhD, quite new to the process of theological education but deeply rooted in the media literacy movement. I was invited into this work by schools that were searching for ways to integrate digital technology into their teaching. For many, this was a process fraught with deep fear and the unsettling feeling that they were entering a context that might refuse to respect their hard-won scholarship and teaching experience.

Far too often I consulted with faculties for whom previous experiences with digital technologies had everything to do with "how" to do something on a computer but that provided no opportunities to discuss "why" it might be important within theological education to respond to digital technology. Few of these teachers had imagined digital technologies as anything other than a computer connected to the Internet. I, on the other hand, cannot conceive of such technologies without seeing the ways in which they are embedded in mass mediated popular culture. To me, theological reflection lives and breathes amidst movies and music, in the interwoven webs of the Internet, and in the daily and quite ordinary ways in which digital technology is built into just about every form of media we now engage. If we are to teach and learn in contemporary culture, we have to engage these media. For me, digital technologies provide a wonderful entry point into popular culture.

As I worked with these faculties, I began to recognize that the same dynamics media literacy educators have struggled with over time—the tendency to assume that media are merely "tools" with which to "push" content to people, for instance—were present in my colleagues' nascent understanding of digital technologies. In addition, many of the teachers with whom I worked had never had the opportunity to reflect on their teaching. Unlike teachers at the primary and secondary levels, these were people whose academic socialization had privileged research and at the same time provided very little access to the depth and abundance of the educational literatures. These graduate theological educators cared deeply about their students and wanted to introduce them to the richness of the theological disciplines but had been given very little idea of the sheer diversity of pedagogical approach that is possible.

I hope that this small book of essays might begin to address these challenges. I have written the essays to stand alone, although they move in sequence. It is my hope that a faculty group might choose one as a jumping-off point for further discussion, a catalyst for reflection on their teaching and learning, and then choose others for follow-up as specific questions become pertinent and interesting to them. Each of these essays provides an entry point into the fascinating and perplexing worlds of digital culture that swirl around and through graduate theological education, but none of them will teach you *how* to use a specific technology. Neither teaching nor technology is best conceived of in instrumental terms. We need to find appropriate ways to express what God has planted within us, and doing so requires that we be as respectful and receptive to our students and colleagues as we can be. I hope that these essays will prove inviting enough to entice even reluctant faculty into bringing their scholarly minds and pedagogical hearts to the task of meeting in deep respect and full presence the students our communities of faith send into our classrooms.

Like any good story, these essays have a narrative arc to them. In chapter 1 I begin with a basic reflection on why theological educators should bother with digital technologies at all. Before we can structure environments for learning, we need to think about what we mean by "knowing" and how learning can support it. Thus, chapter 2 problematizes "knowing" in the context of pop culture's penchant for separating bodies from minds. From there, in chapter 3 I provide some brief reflections geared toward exploring what it means to design learning experiences in theological education. This chapter invites reflection in terms broad enough that even faculties who are not interested in digital technologies should be able to find something with which to engage their imagination as teachers. Only when I have set the stage in this way do I turn to the issues specific to digital technologies. Chapter 4 explores some of the ways in which the construction of particular software shapes the experiences of learning that take place online. Chapter 5 explores what we can learn from previous attempts to integrate emerging technologies into theological education, particularly television, and returns more specifically to the general issues I introduced in chapter 1. Chapter 6 picks up the questions of embodiedness I hear so often in my work with theological faculties. Sometimes it seems to me that the issue faculty are most concerned about is this question of "disembodying" through digital technology. I am convinced that this is an important concern, but I think the question of what is "disembodying" about theological education is one that was raised before digital technologies ever appeared on the radar screen. One of the best ways I know of getting at the roots of the problem is to bring the insights of feminists and others who have engaged issues of race and gender to the table. Thus in chapter 6 I explore their conceptual frameworks to suggest why engaging in antiracist pedagogies can only strengthen our work with digital technologies. Chapter 7 considers issues of copyright and fair use, and chapter 8 provides a set of practical exercises that can be integrated into a variety of courses and which provide a way to engage media cultures without directly using digital technologies.

As any teacher is, I am deeply embedded in the contexts in which I learn. These reflections are situated in my own teaching landscape—a graduate theological school of the ELCA Lutheran tradition. I am a Roman Catholic layperson and thus often find myself moving across various community borders. I am also white, a U.S. citizen, and the parent of two young children. In all of these ways my reflections are limited and meant to be descriptive, not prescriptive. It is my deepest hope that this book will provide a route into collaborative inquiry, helping each of us who teaches in the context of graduate theological education to participate in the exploration of digital technologies now occurring and to bring our best minds, our most open hearts, and our deepest souls to the task.

Chapter One

Rich Treasures in Jars of Clay: Theological Education in Changing Times

Imagine a room full of new seminarians, eager to pick up the tools they'll need for ministry in the twenty-first century. Now imagine a professor, fresh from a summer's reflection, ready to dole out those tools. What's wrong with this picture? Setting aside for the moment whether students or faculty can be "fresh" and eager in a world where they face so many competing demands, focus on the "what" both groups are expecting: students want tools, and faculty expect to give them out.

Every semester in my own context, when I begin the introductory course in Christian education, I face the same dilemma: students enter my classroom eager to pick up and use the most effective tools in religious education, and I have very little to give them. Why? It's not because there aren't piles of wonderful curriculum materials. It's not because I don't know anything about religious education. The dilemma is bigger than tools, it's bigger than assembled knowledge. To be concise: most religious education now takes place in contexts other than those controlled or even designed by religious institutions. Most religious learning takes place in a wider cultural context where even the symbols and stories we place at the heart of our faith are told and interpreted in ways religious communities rarely access, let alone actively engage.

In short we are facing what Ronald Heifetz calls an adaptive challenge. A longtime adult educator, Heifetz has described two kinds of challenges in leadership education: technical and adaptive.

A technical challenge can be illustrated in the following way: A person in pain goes to see a doctor. The doctor diagnoses a broken wrist, puts the person's wrist in a cast, and healing commences. The process of prescribing and implementing the cast is a technical challenge. The extent to which it is successful depends in large measure on the doctor's ability to align the person's wrist bones properly and make the cast well. The patient's responsibility is primarily to interfere as little as possible in the process.

An example of an adaptive challenge goes something as follows: A person in pain goes to see a doctor. After many tests and other consultations, the doctor eventually diagnoses extensive heart disease. In this case there are only a few things the doctor can do technically. The healing challenge here becomes one of supporting the patient in coming to terms with the illness and adapting to the necessary changes in lifestyle. In this case the doctor and the patient together face an adaptive challenge: they must work together in ways that have very little to do with technical skills, but much to do with relationality and meaning-making, with habit and behavior.[1]

I am convinced that the challenges we face right now in supporting teaching and learning in communities of faith in media culture are adaptive challenges, not primarily technical ones. This is nowhere more true than in graduate theological education, where we must encourage our students to become not only fluent and centered participants in Christian communities, but also capable of energetic, critical, and adept leadership there and beyond. We face painful conflicts within our communities—Who is called to leadership? What kind of leadership is appropriate? What does it mean to be a Christian in this time and this place?—but we also face difficult questions that are afloat in the wider cultural contexts that communities of faith inhabit, including questions that arise from the integration of digital technologies into almost all of our daily practices.

Ever since the Lilly Endowment began its generous program of placing digital technologies in seminary settings in the 1990s, I have been an eager participant in questions of theological teaching and learning in and among digital environments. I have watched schools across the country—indeed, globally—begin to place materials on the Web, teach classes in distributed formats, automate various seminary functions such as library catalogs and registrar paperwork—but for the most part I have been disappointed by the extent to which these efforts still mirror the typical formats and pedagogies one would find in standard seminary classrooms. Further, I have witnessed very little discussion of the ethical issues involved, or the social justice questions we ought to be engaging directly.

I think the reason there has been so little of such effort comes back to the question of technical versus adaptive challenges. In theological education we have tended to focus on the technical challenges of digital technologies— what's the right software for course management? What kind of classrooms should we be building? Should PowerPoint be used in lectures, or not? And so on. While these are often very pressing questions, with clear budgetary implications, they are not necessarily the first or the best questions we could be asking.

At the same time as these new digital technologies are flooding into our corridors and libraries, students arrive every year with more and more technical proficiency in the use of these tools, but not necessarily with fluent and centered formation in the community of their faith. Indeed, some commentators have argued that it is precisely the advent of digital technologies that has diluted and made more fragile our religious formation. Here again, another adaptive challenge. Finally, it is unarguably the case that the larger cultural contexts we inhabit in the United States shifted dramatically after the events of September 11, 2001, particularly in relation to the ways in which religious images and religious language suffused popular mass mediated culture.

When the planes hit the World Trade towers on September 11, certain aspects of life as we know it here in the United States changed; for example, most of us, at least for a little while, paid new attention to what was important in our lives. Many of us asked—and continue to ask—new kinds of questions. And some part of our world—a world that here, in the upper Midwest amongst the middle class where I teach, has always been pretty stable and "safe"—appeared more vividly uncertain, more perplexing, and even perhaps more afflicted. It is this combination—of too much focus on the technical challenges, and too little exploration of the adaptive challenges that face us, not simply within theological education but from within our wider, global context as well—that preoccupies me and to which the essays in this book are directed. In this first essay I will "set the stage" for the rest, and seek to invite, in particular, a biblical imagination into the mix.

MADE VISIBLE IN OUR BODIES . . .

Paul writes, in his second letter to the Corinthians: "We are afflicted in every way, but not crushed; perplexed, but not driven to despair; persecuted, but not forsaken; struck down, but not destroyed; always carrying in the body the death of Jesus, so that the life of Jesus may also be made visible in our bodies." This text has new resonance for many of us who have heretofore inhabited worlds of comparative safety and stability, particularly those of us who teach in Christian theological schools that draw our students primarily from white and middle-class U.S. settings. There are many texts in the Bible that are hard to inhabit, difficult to understand, and painful to perform. So much of the biblical witness is a witness to those on the margins, it is a call to protect the *anawim*—orphans, widows, and the alien—it is a language and worldview that makes most sense to those on the "underside" of history. For those of us who inhabit middle-class worlds, for those of us who carry the comparative safety and stability of white skin privilege, for those of us who are U.S. citizens without any effort, I think that Paul's text *means* differently to us, post–September 11.

September 11 was a gift of sorts, not one that I would ever seek, and not one that I would ever wish upon anyone. But still, it was an opportunity for all of us to remember what is important, what is at the heart of our life together, and to renew and revisit a text like Paul's. What does it mean to "always carry in our body the death of Jesus, so that the life of Jesus may also be made visible in our bodies"? Particularly in a context so thoroughly perfused by digital technologies? This is a critical question to carry into any discussion of seminary education, and for now I'd like to use it as a catalyst for considering the challenges involved in supporting teaching and learning within communities of faith. In particular, I'd like to use this text as an opportunity to think about "rescripting theological education for performative practice."

First, I'd like to begin by thinking about the models we have for teaching and learning. What do we think we are doing in communities of faith? What are we about in teaching and learning? Then I'll take a model and use it to think about the script we have for Christian education. What is our script for Christian education in our current contexts? Finally, I'd like to talk about performative practice. Paul exhorts us to "always carry in our body the death of Jesus, so that the life of Jesus may also be made visible in our bodies." Making anything visible in our bodies suggests what I mean by performative practice, and I'd like to work with you on ways to support this kind of teaching and learning, this kind of practice. These are crucial issues that will help to lay a groundwork for meeting the adaptive challenges of digital cultures.

TEACHING AND LEARNING

Anyone who has ever taken part in a dramatic play knows that "in the beginning is the script." Yet, while the script is to govern what the actors engage in, it has only the barest indications of what to do and where to go. Part of what a director does is to help actors think about their motivation for certain actions, as well as to consider the way the whole process works together—when and how actors move in a particular scene, what kinds of props and other physical objects interact, and so on. The script provides some basic and important substance and foundation upon which to build meaning, primarily through dialogue. Then the people who gather—to inhabit the script, to support its action, or to engage its enactment as audience—play with the script to make it come alive. No play can happen without all three—the basic dialogue, the people who seek to inhabit it, and the people who are drawn into meaning-making in watching it unfold. Each time the play is performed, new meanings are created. No two performances are ever alike, and the context in which a play is performed has a crucial impact on its reception.

So, too, with learning. And so, too, with understanding the biblical witness. Paul writes: "we are afflicted in every way, but not crushed; perplexed, but not driven to despair; persecuted, but not forsaken; struck down, but not destroyed." We can begin to imagine some of the context in which he wrote, and we can imagine for ourselves some of what the disciples must have been feeling. But we do not know in any certain way. Simply repeating his words will not help us, because wooden dialogue does not feel real. We must perform it, we cannot simply voice it. It is a pattern of practice, not a stark and systematic statement of belief. It means nothing if we don't allow the script to become part of us to such an extent that we no longer know where the text ends and our lives begin. Learning and teaching within communities of faith ought to carry with it a mandate to support this integral commingling of the divine and human narratives.

Terrence Tilley writes:

> It is hard for Christians . . . to hope for heaven in a culture wherein immediate gratification is the norm, or to understand what holiness of life could be in a culture idolizing conspicuous consumption and material possessions. To believe in heaven and hope for eternal life require participation in a practice or practices that are *not* immediately gratifying. . . . To seek holiness requires participating in practices that shape one's desire *not* to consume and to have "things," but to love God and one's neighbor as oneself. The means are *knowing how* to engage in those patterns of actions and attitudes that seek the goals and carry the vision; mere *knowing that* cannot suffice. Mere notional belief will not do.[2]

We need our teaching and learning in communities of faith to be about *knowing how,* not simply *knowing that.*

There is an important underlying assumption here: that knowing in this way requires participating, that mere information does not equal real knowledge. There is, in other words, an epistemological issue at stake—how we define knowing is crucial to what we mean by teaching and learning. Parker Palmer has written about these questions quite eloquently, and offers a visual model with which to reflect. He argues that we have tended to think of education as a very instrumental and linear process, using what he terms the "objectivist myth of learning" (see fig. 1.1).[3]

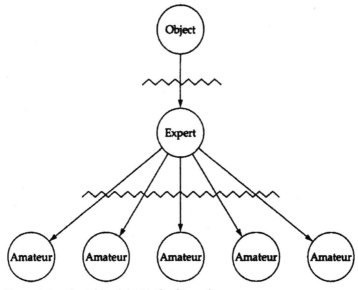

Figure 1.1   The Objectivist Myth of Learning

In this model the "object" of learning is separated from the learners by the mediation of an expert who "takes" information from or about the subject and transfers or imparts it to the amateurs. Teaching and learning become essentially a process of transfer and reception. Teachers transfer information, and students receive it. In this model, it is very clear who the teacher is—the one who provides the bridge for the "pure" content of the subject to the amateurs. It is a very linear process, and the teacher is instrumental to it. Not just because it would not happen without the teacher, but also because the teacher becomes, in effect, an "instrument" by which the information is conveyed. In this model it is very clear that knowledge is something that is transferable via teaching "tools," and you can begin to see how a teacher might be replaced by a computer program or some other machine.

Palmer's second model, by way of contrast, places the subject to be engaged at its center (see fig. 1.2). That is, the thing or things, the ideas or concepts, the feelings and actions that we want to learn from, are at the heart of the process. Palmer calls this the "great thing" around which we gather. Each of us is a knower who is in relationship with the "great thing" that we desire to know, and each of us is also in relationship with each other. Here there are no baffles causing information to flow in only one direction, there are simply multiple ways in which to learn about something, multiple relationships by which we come to know. At the heart of Palmer's model is his assertion that

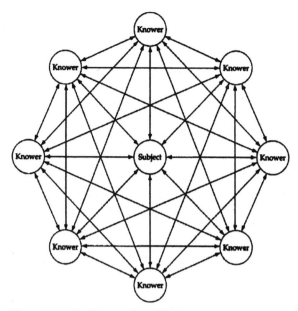

Figure 1.2   The Community of Truth

"we know as we are known." In fact, a marvelous entry point to his thought is the classic little book he titles simply *To Know As We Are Known.*

In this second diagram it is not so clear who the teacher is. Indeed, there are likely many teachers, each with something to share. Perhaps in this model it is more accurate to think of a teacher as someone who is a little bit further down a particular path of learning about the great thing at the heart of the sphere. Someone who can share what she or he has encountered thus far and help others along the path. But it is also accurate in this model to perceive that someone entirely new to the study of the great thing might have something equally important to contribute to the learning and knowing involved.

This model of teaching and learning suggests that knowledge is a dynamic, relational process, rather than a static, isolated quantity. It suggests that the "great thing" in the middle of the diagram might be a script for our participation in the construction of knowledge, as compared to the first model, where knowledge is something isolated from most people and simply transferred through the mediation of a teacher.

This model also has more to contribute to our understanding of *knowing how*, as opposed to *knowing that,* than does the first model. Consider for a moment the ways in which we hear of Jesus teaching. Various gospel authors draw pictures of Jesus in the middle of groups of people, working with their questions, using analogies drawn from the contexts around them, often answering one question with another question. "Who are you?" receives "Who do you say that I am?" "Who is my neighbor?" evokes a story and a question in response. The communities of people who gathered around Jesus were hungry for answers, but they received stories and more questions, and were thereby drawn into new patterns of practice.

If we were to use this model for communities of teaching and learning in seminaries, what would we put at the heart of it? What would be the "great thing" around which we gather? What would be the script we would seek to inhabit? Some scholars have argued that the apostolic script for the church in mission is the biblical witness. When I raise this suggestion with my students, they disagree, arguing that it is obvious that God is at the heart of the diagram, God is the "great thing" around which we gather to learn. Others have suggested that it is some person of the Trinity, Jesus Christ perhaps, or the Holy Spirit. All of these answers have something to commend them, but for me, personally, the biblical witness functions particularly well in this model.

Popular culture—including the "entertainment" offered by our politicians— is rich in examples of ways in which human beings have over time made claims to "know" God, or at the very least, to know what God is communicating to us. Certainly we have very vivid and recent examples in front of us of people who claim to know what God is communicating—so clearly, in fact, that they rejoice in committing other people to following a path that leads to death and destruction.

If we truly do know as we are known, and we put God at the center of the sphere, at the heart of the model as the great thing we gather around, then our conversation is constrained to each of us contributing our perception of who and what God is. This is not a bad thing, and is certainly a powerful and legitimate claim to make for graduate theological education. I think it might even be a good basic description of what we are about when we talk about proclamation.

But I wonder if it is the only way to think about theological education. I wonder if when we talk about teaching and learning in communities of faith we might consider the more limited "great thing" at the heart of our model to be the living tradition of the people of God—found first and foremost in the biblical witness, the text as well as our ongoing encounter with it. Paul writes that "we have this treasure in earthen jars," which in part is why I want to keep the biblical witness at the center of the model. The biblical witness is actually a stream of witnesses, many of which disagree with each other. In other words, it is itself a script for argument.

Kathryn Tanner, a Christian theologian who has spent significant time thinking about the various ways in which we currently conceive of "culture" and then in turn how those conceptions interact with theology, has suggested that "Christian practices are ones in which people participate together in an argument over how to elaborate the claims, feelings, and forms of action around which Christian life revolves."[4]

I have found the single most important question people bring to the biblical witness is precisely this one—what does it mean to "know how" to elaborate the claims, feelings, and forms of action around which Christian life revolves? When we—as teachers and students, followers of Jesus in a seminary—struggle to understand a particular biblical passage, it is not primarily, or ever only, for the abstract purposes of contributing to scholarly archives somewhere, but because we want to inhabit this script, we want its language and ideas to become our own. The kinds of questions raised within communities of faith these days are not over whether or not to have the biblical witness as our script, but *how* to do so.

What would it mean to use Palmer's model and put the biblical witness at the center as our script for Christian practice? I can immediately hear some of my more orthodox Lutheran students objecting—"we can't do that, that would be works righteousness!" So before I go any further, let me be clear that what I am proposing here is larger than a specific definition of Christian practice centered on some form of "doing" for salvation. It is, instead, an assertion that teaching and learning communities can be reinvigorated by having at their heart the "great thing" that is a conscious and intentional engagement with the argument of what Christian practice is and how we are to engage it, that is, with the biblical witness. This is not a definition that precludes proclamation, it is simply a focused definition of Christian education, and a definition that invites sustained scholarship in precisely the areas that seminaries traditionally work. This definition of Christian education honors the distinct and specific ways in which various Christian communities have struggled over time. It suggests, for instance, that there is something around which Christian life revolves (there is a script!), and yet it leaves how we embody that script to be specified by the arguments in which we engage as we think through, work through, pray through our ways of being in the world. It is a model for Christian *learning*, above all else. And it provides a way to engage our differences as crucial insight, crucial knowing. If we are all knowers, all teachers and learners, and if the great thing we put at the heart of our study is an ongoing argument over Christian practice, then arguing is not only possible, but life-giving and liberating.

We need not fear our differences but take encouragement from the ways in which they heighten our insights and provide room for multiple images of Christian life to emerge. Conflict over ideas would be welcomed as a way to clarify them. Indeed, Parker Palmer has another quote that I think is relevant here. He writes that when we practice this form of teaching and learning, this putting of "great things" at the heart of our scripts:

> We invite *diversity* into our community not because it is politically correct but because diverse viewpoints are demanded by the manifold mysteries of great things. We embrace *ambiguity* not because we are confused or indecisive but because we understand the inadequacy of our concepts to embrace the vastness of great things. We welcome *creative conflict* not because we are angry or hostile but because conflict is required to correct our biases and prejudices about the nature of great things. We practice *honesty* not only because we owe it to one another but because to lie about what we have seen would be to betray the truth of great things. We experience *humility* not because we have fought and lost but because humility is the only lens through which great things can be seen—and once we have seen them, humility is the only posture possible.[5]

I cannot think of a better way to put Paul's admonition that "we have this treasure in clay jars" at the heart of our learning than to practice what Palmer calls the grace of great things.

Indeed, if we put the biblical witness at the heart of our model, if we say that the script we are trying to make come alive is "an argument over how to elaborate the claims, feelings, and forms of action around which Christian life revolves," then it is not only Christians who may be a part of this argument, but those beyond our immediate self-defined community as well. I have been most challenged by the biblical witness as it finds itself performed in multiple cultures, in different languages and locations. I have learned crucial lessons about Christianity from people who are not themselves Christian—particularly those who have been the subject of systematic persecution at the hands of Christians. I am also very conscious—as must be anyone who has been awake during the great public debate of Mel Gibson's film *The Passion of the Christ*—of how much the argument over what it is to be Christian is contested in popular mass media.

At the same time, such a script for Christian education does not relativize everything, because it appropriately proclaims that there is a center around which we gather, there is a tradition to which we crave access and in which we desire to live our lives fully. A center from which we desire to share light and love with others. Putting this script at the heart of our teaching and learning communities provides enormous room for inquiry—we can think in historical terms: who are the people of God and how have they understood who God is and who they are becoming in relation to God? We can think in biblical terms: what are the central themes placed in front of us in the biblical witness? How have we engaged these ideas over time? How have we told and retold these stories? We can think in theological terms: what are the implications of a particular Christian practice for our understanding of God? We can think in liturgical terms: how do changing worship practices shift our understanding of God?

These are all ways in which seminaries, for instance, have structured our communities of inquiry. But this script for teaching and learning in communities of faith has much wider ramifications, because it also suggests that we can ask what our own lives might contribute to these questions. What does popular culture contribute to our way of understanding the biblical witness, for instance? Recently, popular culture has been full of contestation over that question. Mel Gibson's film *The Passion of the Christ* opened to a box office that has seen few equals. The television drama *Joan of Arcadia*, which portrays a teenage girl who regularly converses with God, was one of the new hit series. The song "Where Is the Love?" essentially a prayer, hit the top ten lists and was nominated for a Grammy award. All of these examples are part of an ongoing argument that is taking place in our culture right now. What it means to inhabit the biblical witness as a script for our participation is a crucial question. A question whose answers are being worked out in many, many places—many of which are not in any way linked to historically grounded religious institutions. What can we do about this? Here is where combining Palmer's second model, the collaborative description of teaching and learning, with a new sense of the biblical witness as a script for our participation becomes so useful.

What is involved in preparing to perform a play? What do we need to do? First, we certainly need to begin by learning our script! But learning a script entails far more than memorizing words. Wooden, parroted dialogue does not in any way feel real. We need to explore the contexts in which the words were written, we need to imagine the motivations and feelings behind them, and we need to explore our way into making them our own. This is a collaborative process, and itself involves the argument at the heart of our model—how *do* we elaborate the claims, feelings, and forms of action around which Christian life revolves? Who are the learners and teachers in this process? Each and every one of us. Among us there will be people who have been walking in pilgrimage along this path for some time and will have much to share. And there will be people who are brand new, just hearing the words for the first time—they, too, will bring crucial insight.

Second, we need to practice performing. Please understand, the metaphor I'm playing with right now is not meant to see practice itself as salvific. But it does suggest that *knowing how* is more important than simply *knowing that*. Many fresh attempts are being made to explore this kind of "knowing how" based on issues of practice. The work of the Valparaiso Project on the Education and Formation of People in Faith is particularly popular in arenas beyond the seminary, but I find that my students are often moved by their work as well.

Remember what Paul writes:

> We are afflicted in every way, but not crushed; perplexed, but not driven to despair; persecuted, but not forsaken; struck down, but not destroyed; always carrying in the body the death of Jesus, so that the life of Jesus may also be made visible in our bodies.

After September 11 those of us who usually inhabit middle-class privilege may now *feel* our ways into Paul's words more adequately, more deeply. I believe we may know more of how it feels to be perplexed but not driven to despair. But we still need to practice "always carrying in the body the death of Jesus, so that the life of Jesus may also be made visible in our bodies."

Actors preparing to enact a play practice over and over again in multiple contexts, sometimes on their own but more often with their collaborators. Sometimes with minimal sets and costumes, and eventually with a full and complete dress rehearsal. But with any play the practice is not the whole event, because it's not truly whole until there is also an audience engaged in participation. The audience brings the context alive and participates in hearing and making meaning out of the dialogue. No matter how well and how hard the actors have practiced, the audience can and does change the meaning of what is happening.

This brings me to my third point in how it is we can begin to inhabit the biblical witness as the script at the heart of our communities of teaching and learning. We have to enact this script in multiple contexts, in as many as we can enter into. This is an imperative for evangelism, for mission in the best sense of the word. Not because we seek in any way to impose our script on others, but because we know, deep in our bones, deep in our souls, that we can only really *know* this script with as wide a circle of fellow learners as possible. This model that Palmer describes only strengthens Paul's words that "everything is for your sake, so that grace, as it extends to more and more people, may increase thanksgiving, to the glory of God." Where two or three are gathered there is indeed learning and teaching, but where the sphere extends to embrace many more, there is that much more potential for participating in deep knowing. It is not surprising that seminaries across the United States are reconfiguring our curriculum strategies, rewriting our mission statements to understand our goal as being an apostolate, oriented outward in mission, rather than inward in study alone.

This practice of learning in conversation with difference is crucial with respect to the biblical witness in particular. Scholars invite participants from the past into our midst, helping us to nuance and understand myriad resonances of the script that we might otherwise miss, given our ignorance of the original languages. But it is not just the past that we need to invite. In my travels I have had the opportunity to visit Thailand, and while I was there I learned the story of a young Jesuit who died reaching out to embrace an angry and embittered landmine victim, a young child who carried a bomb into the midst of a school. Religious communicators in Southeast Asia have produced a powerful film about this event, and the text on which it centers—"there is no greater love than to lay down one's life for a friend"—means something much deeper and more whole for me, having encountered it in that community.[6]

I noted earlier that so much of the biblical witness is oriented to the margins, to the *anawim*—those who are poor, who are orphaned, who are widowed, who are aliens. Biblical texts are heard differently, performed differently, inhabited differently, in different contexts. We can extend and enrich our own practice and our own knowing by embracing in respectful dialogue all those who seek to live from this script. Like any argument, however, and remember that I have suggested that the biblical witness is at heart also a powerful argument, there will be interpreters who will perform this script in ways that we cannot and must not condone. When the state church in Germany saw the biblical witness as condoning Hitler, it forced other Christians—and those beyond the Christian community—to object. Even our own contemporary religious institutions are only, as Paul notes, "clay jars" into which this powerful witness is poured. One of the best ways to maintain our humility, to practice the grace of great things I noted earlier, is to require ourselves to try and do so in as many contexts and with as many partners as possible.

Finally, I think there is a fourth thing we can do. Once we have learned our script, practiced it, performed it in many different contexts, I think we also begin to learn how to improvise with it. People I know who are involved with improvisational theater tell me that it is crucial to know the moves and gestures that convey meaning, to know how scripts work so deeply in your being that you can perform even when the script is being changed or you are inventing it as you play. The circumstances around us, the contexts in which we live, are changing rapidly. So rapidly that some commentators say we live in a perpetual state of "blur." Others write that we must learn to live by navigating constant whitewater. Whatever the image you use, increasingly we have to recognize that we are being called upon to practice improvisation. Business leaders are responding to these rapidly changing contexts by transforming their businesses into learning organizations. They are creating ways for their employees to make ongoing learning a continual part of their work lives. Can we afford to do anything less within a community of faith?

These four efforts—learning our script, practicing it, performing it in multiple contexts, learning to improvise—take on greater urgency when the contexts are always changing around us. One primary context in which we learn and teach right now is mass-mediated popular culture—from movies and television to news and documentaries; from books and magazines to the World Wide Web. As a seminary educator you might not think of popular culture as a medium in which you learn, let alone teach, but what did you do when you first heard of what was going on in New York on September 11, 2001? You probably turned on your radio or your television set, or logged on to the Web. For days following September 11, you could find clusters of people gathered around communication technologies. It used to be that people would gather in their local churches for such news. Such gatherings still occurred during that week in September of 2001, and in some cases even for weeks afterward. Now, three years later, the church/synagogue attendance figures have dropped off again, and yet we still turn to our global communications network.

Some people might be quite pessimistic about the health of communities of faith in this kind of context, but I'm actually optimistic. To begin with, in some of the same ways in which I'm asking you to shift your understanding of teaching and learning from an instrumental to a more collaborative notion, scholars have begun to rewrite their models for how mass mediated popular culture works. That is, instead of seeing mass media as pipelines through which messages are piped directly into our passive brains, scholars are increasingly noting the extent to which people play with, resist, contest, and even ignore mass mediated messages.

The same Palmer diagram I used to talk about collaborative teaching and learning can be used to describe the ways in which people engage mass media. There is room, then, for imagining that the teaching and learning communities that we grow in congregations can engage media culture as an essential resource for knowledge, that it could be, even, a source upon which we draw to "know as we are known." The key, though, is understanding the ways in which some of the scripts provided for our attention there give us practice in performances that are at odds with the biblical witness.

Brian Eno (a songwriter and performance artist) writes that "familiarity breeds content. When you use familiar tools, you draw upon a long cultural conversation—a whole shared history of usage—as your backdrop, as the canvas to juxtapose your work. The deeper and more widely shared the conversation, the more subtle its inflections can be." Right now mass mediated popular culture is something our students are much more familiar with than most of the biblical witness. And increasingly, given how hungry people are for meaning in their lives, even mass mediated popular culture is presenting to us parts of the biblical witness. Avril Lavigne, in a hit song released in 2002 entitled "Complicated," sang that "life's like this . . . you fall and you crawl and you take what you get and you turn it into honesty." I have no idea if she had religious imagery in mind as she wrote that song, but I know that the students I've shared that song with have found it a vivid resource for thinking about grace and about the ways in which forgiveness and reconciliation might function.[7]

We can and must, as members of teaching and learning communities who are preparing leaders for congregations, enter into popular culture, into mass mediated contexts precisely to draw on this long cultural conversation. We can work with this shared history to broaden our conversation and to make our own learning that much more complex and subtle. In the process, however, we will need to pay attention to the ways in which the mass mediated conversation is narrow, the ways in which the conversation is exclusive rather than inclusive, the ways in which this mass mediated conversation focuses on some things and completely ignores others. This is, of course, the same kind of concern we must have in relation to learning in other contexts. We are human, and we carry our witness in the earthen jars of which Paul speaks.

In a moment in time in which "wardrobe malfunctions" and "shock jock radio" occupy more of our attention than the millions of people who are hungry and without shelter in the United States—let alone the myriad issues that we ignore of our connection in the global village—it is crucial that communities of faith, and seminaries more narrowly (as we invite and nurture leaders for such communities), find ways to truly see for ourselves the kinds of dynamics at work in our larger cultural spheres.[8] In part we can do so by inhabiting fully a different script and performing it in those same cultural spheres. This is not an argument for creating a separate sphere—which in any case I don't believe is possible—but rather it is an argument for living and improvising in our current contexts with richer resources to draw upon, with a different script to use.

Let's go back to Paul again:

> We are afflicted in every way, but not crushed; perplexed, but not driven to despair; persecuted, but not forsaken; struck down, but not destroyed; always carrying in the body the death of Jesus, so that the life of Jesus may also be made visible in our bodies. For while we live, we are always being given up to death for Jesus' sake, so that the life of Jesus may be made visible in our mortal flesh.

This is a very different image of security than that fed to us through the performances of advertising, for example. But we need to know more than *that* it is different, we need to know *how* to live into the differences.

Here again is a question that we can take to the heart of our learning and teaching sphere, to the great thing which is the biblical witness, which is the living tradition of the people of God, and inquire: How do we learn to live in this way? How do we learn to live in such a way that we love God and our neighbors as ourselves? I want to return to an idea I lifted up at the very beginning of this essay—that these questions exemplify an adaptive challenge rather than a technical one. If it were simply a technical challenge, there would be ten tips and tricks for coming to a better practice of love (or for that matter, of theological education that helps people "know how"). But responding to an adaptive challenge requires something else.

First, it requires a new learning model that allows us to imagine different possibilities within our central script. I hope you've been persuaded by my suggestion of what we could use as this new model, or if not persuaded, at least have been willing to entertain the idea. Second, in living with this collaborative model of teaching and learning, these emerging suggestions for ways in which to inhabit the script of the biblical witness, we need to shape our attention differently. Ronald Heifetz, who as I mentioned earlier identified this idea of technical versus adaptive challenge, argues that the work of leadership requires helping people pay disciplined attention to the challenge, to keep it on a "low simmer." In other words, if attention becomes too focused on the challenge, people flee to authority and lose their own investment and capability of response; or they do the opposite and flee into denial.

It is possible to discern these temptations—of a flight to authority or denial of problems—right in the heart of our current context post–September 11. It is certainly very tempting to give up our own reasoned judgment in favor of accepting whatever the government wants to do, or to back away from the fears and dilemmas altogether and simply pretend that life continues on as before.

The same thing has happened within the Christian community, however, in relation to the biblical witness. This script that we need to inhabit, this great thing at the heart of our community, raises far more questions than it answers; it poses far more difficult dilemmas—especially for those of us who live relatively powerful, wealthy existences relative to the rest of God's creation. It is far too easy, as a member of a congregation, to appeal to church leaders to interpret the script, to compartmentalize it to a Sunday morning performance, or to ignore it completely.

What does it mean to hold this kind of focus? Neither too sharp nor too fuzzy? Neither too close nor out of sight? It is not something that we can do alone. It is something that must be done in community. It is not something that can be done in instrumental terms—there is no expert that can give us the technical fix—rather, we need to find multiple ways to focus and challenge our attention. Sharon Parks, one of a group of a scholars who did a major study several years ago about the factors that support people's commitment to the common good, writes that one of the important factors her team identified was the ability to sustain a responsible imagination. In Parks's words:

> Living with these images, the people in our study appear to know that two truths must be held together—that we have the power to destroy the Earth and the power to see it whole. But unlike many who seek escape from the potent tension this act of holding requires, these people live in a manner that conveys a third and essential power: the courage to turn and make promises, the power of a responsible imagination.[9]

Here is Paul again:

> We are afflicted in every way, but not crushed; perplexed, but not driven to despair; persecuted, but not forsaken; struck down, but not destroyed; always carrying in the body the death of Jesus, so that the life of Jesus may also be made visible in our bodies. For while we live, we are always being given up to death for Jesus' sake, so that the life of Jesus may be made visible in our mortal flesh.

Living in this way requires the ability to attend to these paradoxes without being overcome by them. Living in this way requires a creative tension, it requires a certain kind of "simmer"—it is, indeed, an adaptive challenge, particularly in our contemporary media culture. Why is it so difficult in the larger American context? Why are we so driven to compartmentalize? To flee into authority or into denial?

Attention is one of our most precious resources in contemporary U.S. culture. You can see this in the most crass terms by noticing how many billions of dollars are spent each year attempting to "capture" our attention. In a world that functions with a global communications network, in a world that promises near instant satisfaction of curiosity, in a world that turns even human desire into a commodity to be marketed to the highest bidder, sustaining focused attention that can tolerate tension is not easy.

There is no technical "fix" that can be applied, no Bible study, no media literacy curriculum, no single "type" of worship. We are not in need of a well-placed cast. We need to revitalize our congregations as communities of teaching and learning that hold at their heart the goal of truly performing the script of the biblical witness. And at the heart of that adaptive challenge is a struggle over our attention. You may think that that struggle focuses on content, but I am convinced it has far more to do with the practices by which we structure our attention.

If Christian theological education uses a collaborative model, and if we place at the heart of that model our script of the biblical witness, then I think we have to notice that popular media structure most of our forms of attention, in ways that we barely even notice anymore—indeed, in ways to which we do not "pay attention." We are enacting scripts we've learned so well that we have to work hard to see them in a different light, let alone to attempt to perform a different script in the same context.

More and more of the compelling religious questions we face in our culture—and hence more and more of the learning that takes place—are being broached in popular media culture. But theologians have thus far focused on the challenges of media culture in much the same way that we have conceived of learning—instrumentally. We have worried about electronic screens and we have worried about the content of popular culture, and in doing so we have sought to figure out how to have either a better "technique" for conveying our own content, or how to have a better way of inoculating people against the dangerous content carried by the electronic pipelines. Yet each of these worries assumes that mass media work in instrumental ways and, even more so, assume an instrumental model of teaching and learning. They assume that religious experts can and must control the performance of our shared script. Neither of these assumptions is adequately descriptive of the world we inhabit. We need at one and the same time to let go of our perceived control over that witness and to be even more engaged in living into it.

We cannot succeed by asking everyone to participate only in "Christian approved" content or by asking everyone to boycott problematic "secular" content. In doing so we force people into narrow enclaves of Christian identity, or we force them into vast trivialization of Christian truths. We force them to flee either to authority or to denial. This cannot be what we mean by Christian identity, and it does us no good to conceive of teaching and learning, let alone apostolic mission, in these narrow ways. We need to think about the ways in which we can invite religious resonance that is always and everywhere present, that is clearly woven into our lives every day and in every way. We need to find a way to respond to the Holy Spirit's invitation to play. We need to find a way to live into the script of the biblical witness, to make it our own. We need to find a way to engage a responsible imagination, one that helps us to keep our attention at a low simmer, to be "afflicted in every way, but not crushed; perplexed, but not driven to despair." One that helps us to have the courage to turn and to make promises.

We need to nurture communities of teaching and learning, communities of ministry that help members to identify and share their gifts; communities that help people to voice their vocations and attend to them wherever they are drawn; communities that help people to collaborate across multiple forms of knowing, multiple intelligences, in the search for the "claims, feelings, and forms of action around which Christian life revolves."

For while we live, we are always being given up to death for Jesus' sake, so that the life of Jesus may be made visible in our mortal flesh.

We need to live in such a way—performatively—that this exhortation of Paul's rings true, and we need to teach and learn in such a way that we can support people in keeping their attention at a simmer. If familiarity truly does breed content, then we have to begin to help people become familiar with the deeper structures of our faith, with the arguments that we engage in because they matter to us—hence why and how they matter to us. And to do so we need to develop a responsible imagination.

In the rest of the essays in this book, I invite you to focus your attention, stimulate your imagination, and consider the ways in which digital cultures—the media in which most of our popular culture exists—can become a part of our teaching and learning practices in seminaries. We must bring all that we can to bear in developing this kind of responsible imagination and actively putting it to work on "elaborating the claims, feelings, and forms of action around which Christian life revolves."

FOR FURTHER REFLECTION

Books

Hoover, Stewart. "The Culturalist Turn in Scholarship on Media and Religion." *Journal of Media and Religion* 1, no. 1 (2002): 25–36.

Hoover, Stewart, Lynn Clark, and Diane Alters. *Media, Home, and Family.* New York and London: Routledge, 2004.

Hoover, Stewart, and Lynn Clark, eds. *Practicing Religion in an Age of Media.* New York: Columbia University Press, 2002.

Mitchell, Jolyon, and Sofia Marriage, eds. *Mediating Religion: Conversations in Media, Religion, and Culture.* Edinburgh: T & T Clark; New York: Continuum, 2003.

Stout, Daniel, and Judith Buddenbaum, eds. *Religion and Popular Culture: Studies on the Interaction of Worldviews.* Ames: University of Iowa Press, 2001.

Whiteley, Raewynne, and Beth Maynard. *Get Up off Your Knees: Preaching the U2 Catalog.* Cambridge, MA: Cowley Publications, 2003.

Films

Bend It Like Beckham. DVD. Directed by Gurinder Chadha. Twentieth Century Fox Home Video, 2003.

Rabbit Proof Fence. DVD. Directed by Phillip Noyce. Miramax Home Entertainment, 2004.

Whale Rider. DVD. Directed by Niki Caro. Columbia Tristar Homevideo, 2003.

Multimedia CD-ROMs

The Mediated Spirit. CD-ROM. Written and created by Peter Horsfield. Commission for Mission, Uniting Church in Australia, 2003. More information available at: www.mediatedspirit.com (accessed on May 13, 2004).

Ministry in a Multi-cultural World: Beyond Borders. CD-ROM. Written and created by Adán Medrano. JMCommunications.com, 2003. More information available at: www.maccsa.org/Merchant2/merchant.mv?Screen=PROD&Store_Code=maccsa &Product_Code=0932545122 (accessed on May 13, 2004).

NOTES

1. Ronald Heifetz, *Leadership without Easy Answers* (Cambridge: Harvard University Press, 1994), 73–84.

2. Terrence Tilley, *Inventing Catholic Tradition* (Maryknoll, NY: Orbis Books, 2000), 78.

3. This figure, and the following, are taken from Parker Palmer, *The Courage to Teach: Exploring the Inner Landscape of a Teacher's Life* (San Francisco: Jossey-Bass, 1998), 100. Reprinted by permission of John Wiley & Sons.

4. Kathryn Tanner, *Theories of Culture: A New Agenda for Theology* (Minneapolis: Fortress Press, 1997), 125.

5. Palmer, *The Courage to Teach,* 107–8.

6. The video, entitled *Greater Love*, is dedicated to the memory of the young Jesuit, Richie Fernando, and can be acquired by writing to Sonolux Bldg., Ateneo de Manila University, Loyola Heights, Quezon City, Philippines (jcf@pusit.admu.edu.ph).

7. Avril Lavigne, "Complicated," from the album *Let Go*, compact disc (Arista, 2002).

8. As I write this, the U.S. Federal Communications Commission is calling for hearings on the public "failure" of Janet Jackson's costume, which bared her breast during the Super Bowl, and for inquiries into Howard Stern's radio show.

9. Laurent A. Parks Daloz, Cheryl H. Keen, James P. Keen, and Sharon Daloz Parks, *Common Fire: Lives of Commitment in a Complex World* (Boston: Beacon Press, 1996), 152.

Chapter Two

Searching for the Blue Fairy: Questioning Technology and Pedagogy in Theological Education

Many of us as small children learned the story of Pinocchio and the beautiful Blue Fairy who granted him life as a "real boy." In recent years the Blue Fairy has reappeared in a number of incarnations in popular culture, but one of the more vivid for me, personally, was the frozen, broken statue at the base of flooded New York City near the end of the movie *A.I.*[1] In that film, David, a young robot, or "mecha" (for mechanical), sets out on a quest that consumes the movie: how can he become real? For David, that question is bound up with what it is to be human, and therein lies the center of the film. Although the film was not a box office success, perhaps because its messages were too complex for easy consumption, nonetheless Steven Spielberg created a profound meditation on this question—"What does it mean to be human?"—and he did so in peculiarly embodied terms.

Margaret Miles has argued that in this time and in our mass mediated cultural contexts, we tend to explore pressing public issues in our pop films.[2] If that is so, then it is clear that the question of what it means to be human is raised in some very compelling ways by our digital technologies—a reality that Spielberg is picking up on in this film. Asking what it means to be human—particularly in relation to God—is also at the foundation, if not the heart, of much theological reflection. As graduate institutions of theological education engage digital technologies, we need to hear the depth of this question; not just in our immediate contexts, but in the larger cultural settings of which we are also a part. Hearing these themes, engaging them, acting upon them—this is what I meant by the dramatic metaphors I employed in my first chapter. The other structure I used there circled around the issue of "technical" versus "adaptive" challenges.

In this chapter I want to return to the notion of adaptive challenge and place on the table several of the questions we need to engage within theological education. Let me be clear: I do not pretend to have adequate answers to these challenges. I do, however, have some frameworks to offer for engaging them, and often a couple of good questions and several frameworks for analysis can take us further together than we could possibly have walked alone.

At the heart of some of the most vivid debates within theological education is the question of "knowing"—what constitutes knowing? Who is a knower? What do we mean by knowledge? These questions are raised in multiple contexts, in multiple ways, by multiple people. I cannot possibly hope to engage all of them here. But I can ask us to step back for a moment and note that these epistemological inquiries extend far beyond the seminary, or even the academy: they are at the heart of popular culture.

Films such as *A.I.* pose the question of what it is to be human in terms that contrast an "instrumental" or a controlling "for the use of" notion of human being with an "expressive" or "in relationship" notion of human being. The debates about genetic research, or fertility manipulation, or patenting of gene maps also raise these issues of instrumental versus expressive understandings of human being: is science to be governed solely by profit motives, for instance, or might we believe that there are some limits as to what we do, technologically, with the basic science we pursue?

As Mary Boys points out, every definition of religious education (including more narrow descriptions of graduate theological education) defines how humans know, whether such descriptions do so consciously and intentionally, or incidentally and unintentionally.[3] Who are we in relation to God? How do I know God? How do I know myself? What is real? Who is my neighbor? and so on. These are familiar and ancient questions at the heart of Jesus' own pedagogical practices. But they are also questions that are popping up vividly all over mass mediated popular culture: *The X-Files, A.I., The Matrix, The Truman Show, Pleasantville, Galaxy Quest*. All of these are recent television shows or films that explore such questions, albeit not generally in theological terms.

But there is a version of the question that is not so often directly stated, and which is deeply implicated in our discussion about digital technologies and theological education. That is the question of what it means to be human in the process of learning. How do humans know? What are the limits to human knowing? How do we support human knowledge through learning? How do we increase knowledge? and so on. The process of integrating digital technologies into theological education raises these foundational questions anew, because there are myriad ways in which we are facing new choices, new possibilities.

The advent of the Web, for instance, and with it the ability to take teaching and learning out of our typical classrooms and practice it in a way that erases time and ignores geography, has brought some particularly thorny dilemmas front and center. We profess faith in an incarnational God—what does it mean to engage a technology that perhaps urges us to ignore our own embodiedness? Isn't the practice of ministry a fundamentally relational process, and so shouldn't our teaching of it be that, too? Does technology urge us to ignore our embodiedness? Or can it make our relationality more tangible? Does digital technology erase our humanity, or make our common bonds more visible?

These are crucial questions for all of us to ask, but I am impatient with some of the rush to simplistic answers. Rather than assuming that online distributive formats are disembodied, for instance, or that our most familiar forms of pedagogy in typical classrooms are also our most fully embodied pedagogies, I'd like us to pause and consider the questions more deeply.

How do we "know" what we know? What do we confess about what it is to be human and embodied? And how does that confession—which takes specific shape in different communities—shape our teaching and learning? Answers to these questions might begin to describe what an embodied pedagogy that is faithful to God should look like. It may be coincidental, although I doubt it, but new—and in some ways surprisingly similar—questions about how human beings know and how we learn are emerging across the literatures of education in relation to neuroscience. Just as digital technologies make new possibilities available in graduate theological education, they create new opportunities for measuring brain activity while learning. Can what we are learning about how the brain works, about how the mind processes sensory information, also help us to understand how we learn, and then how we teach? These questions are now being asked in relation to religious experience and the mind. Surprisingly, the answers—while framed in new discourses that draw heavily on neuroscience—point to learning and teaching practices that have long been effective. Again, it is perhaps the questions asked in new frameworks that awaken us to resources we can retrieve from our traditions.

At Luther Seminary, for example, my own most immediate teaching context, we have observed the Lutheran Church becoming more and more marginal— even in the middle of the upper Midwest, where I am assured that vestiges of Christendom still remain. In observing this cultural shift we have asked ourselves how it has come about and what we can do about it. Part of our answer lies in recognizing that some of the organic linkages that once bound local communities of faith and our seminary have been weakened, in some cases attenuated to such a degree that they are no longer tangible.

Our understanding of what it means to be church, particularly church as the people gathered, as the body of God, needs to be renewed. And so we have committed ourselves to a missional understanding of our enterprise. We have embarked on radically reshaping our educational process so that it is deeply contextual. We are building frameworks in which students will learn in the context of the local neighborhood, not just in the context of the seminary; where our teachers will be drawn from the ranks of practicing leaders, not solely practicing academics. We have begun to understand our "body" in ways quite different from how we have done so in the twentieth century but are actually more deeply linked to earlier Christian understandings. And we have begun to experiment with the ways in which the Internet—usually most specifically the Web—can help us to overcome the constraints of time and geographic location.

In this case, asking what it is to be human and embodied has led us to respond, in part, that it means to be relational and to be members of the Body of Christ. From this perspective, using digital technologies in our teaching should grow out of a desire to build communities of learning that visibly demonstrate the global nature of the Body of Christ, that tangibly gather knowledge from diverse corners of the Christian community. What is fascinating to me is that the answers we are arriving at in experimenting—answers that come more from intuition, from trial and error while exploring new digital tools, from asking pedagogical questions of these tools—these answers sound remarkably similar to what scientists tell teachers who ask what we might do with what they are learning about how the brain shapes knowing and learning. Are the tools shaping our learning and knowing? Are we arriving at answers embedded in the very questions we ask? Of course. Does that make the answers any less useful? I doubt it, as long as we remain ever self-critical and focused on expressive and transformative learning rather than instrumental "transmitting" of information.

But how might we do so, particularly in the contexts of graduate theological education? For the rest of this essay I'd like to integrate voices into the discussion that come from a digital text. The text is entitled *Beyond Borders: Ministry in the Multicultural Context,* and was produced and developed at the MACC in San Antonio.[4] In doing so I am not trying to imply that one can only engage these questions using digital technologies, but rather I hope to invite you, the reader, into such discussion *with* digital technologies. Inasmuch as this is a print text, I have to do that by quoting specific people who were interviewed for the CD-ROM. It is widely available, however, and I hope this essay invites you to find a copy and listen and view the interviews in their entirety.

Let me begin with Dr. Gloria Lloyd, who notes:

The challenge . . . [is that] . . . in the U.S. very often there's a split between what is conceived as the practical, or praxis, the pastoral, and in the U.S. what is considered academic. And as Latinos, we're sometimes caught between those two things, which is really inconceivable because the two go together. . . . How do we keep these together, that's a real challenge . . . how do I keep staying in touch with my people, not just thinking, over here in this other place, but truly, bodily, when do I take time from my teaching, but also to be with the people and accompany them? . . . how do we go forward in this mestizo theology, integrating these two very important realms?[5]

This understanding of learning community requires us to support teachers and learners whose lives prevent their knowledge construction from being confined to a nine-to-five residential campus. It also invites us into the recognition that Parker Palmer so beautifully states, that learning is about practicing "the grace of great things." This is a way of understanding teaching and learning that at its heart is profoundly transformative rather than simply transmissive (as the diagrams in chapter 1 point out).

This way of understanding community—and the learning that grows within it—can also be found at the heart of recent descriptions of how one can "enrich the practice of teaching by exploring the biology of learning," to use James Zull's phrase. As he notes:

Our exploration of the biology of learning has reminded us of many things we already knew but has also given us a deeper respect for the learner and the learning process. Repeatedly we have been reminded that it is our physical body and its interactions with the physical world that produce learning . . . "[6]

In writing about the implications of that learning, Zull repeatedly returns to key phrases like "attending," "sense luscious," "test by trial and action," "play," "stories," "authenticity," and so on. Whether one wants to use the language of neuronal pathways or embodied spirituality, the implications are similar: our learning is deeply embodied and contextual. That is, learning takes place within individual bodies, but those bodies are not isolated but, rather, deeply embedded in various contexts that make learning a highly relational process.

In our current mass mediated contexts, this understanding is often embedded in film. As teachers who want to make that learning come alive, it is often better to work *from* such an understanding *to* the abstract concepts involved, rather than vice versa. As Zull notes about one of his students, "when he understood how things worked, Tim asked for the names. And the names came to symbolize concepts. . . . First he created meaning, and *then* he needed vocabulary."[7]

Asking what it means to be embodied, and then how learning can be nurtured in noninstrumental ways, requires us to rethink our understanding of how technologies work and how learning happens with them. In the film *A.I.*, it is the robots, or "mechas," who can collaborate with each other, who know how to physically respond with care and attention, who have some critical perspective on their situation, who evidence learning. The "orgas" (short for organic), on the other hand, are pretty much people without emotional insight, so caught up in their feelings that they either must deny them by sublimating them in their intellectual work (as does the scientist who creates David), or give way to them, enjoying the ramped up fear and mass energy of the "flesh fair," a kind of Roman circus where old mechas are taken to be destroyed in a highly inventive and supposedly entertaining fashion.

I confess that watching this film reminded me anew of all the reasons why modernist thought worked to move beyond affective frames of knowing, strove to find a universal perspective from which to critically engage and construct knowledge. So many theological school faculty worry about the disembodied nature of digital technologies in learning, but I suspect we ought to worry equally about learning that is focused solely on the affective to the denial of cognitive issues.

The film *A.I.*, like *The Matrix* before it (another recent film full of religious analogies), worries that human beings can be captured by our emotions rather than learning to sense reality through them. And the central symbol of that captivity these films present are our forms of entertainment. Yet these films are themselves examples of "entertainment." What are they problematizing, and what can we learn from it? Is there a deeper understanding of the word "entertainment" here? Perhaps one that builds on its root meaning of "betweenness"? Both *A.I.* and *The Matrix* are films that "work" with us on emotional as well as intellectual levels. They are films that repay our engagement with them. So perhaps part of the message is that there is a delicate balance involved, a creative tension necessary, between ideas and feelings.

Jesus taught using metaphors, images, ideas from his local, daily context. But his parables are not easy to understand. If you "get them" on the first take, you've probably missed some aspect of their meaning. I'm not trying to argue that digital media are directly equivalent to parables, but perhaps, analogous to parables, they require us to reflect affectively as well as cognitively. Jesus' parables went a step further: beyond just engaging our ideas and our feelings, they also invite us to live in a certain way—to act upon what we've learned. I am convinced that learning the practices of ministry requires this multiple engagement. Ministry is an embodied practice, so it is not surprising that theological educators should wonder and worry about how we practice teaching and learning as embodied disciplines. Terrence Tilley, in his book *Inventing*

Catholic Tradition, argues that traditions are neither "made" nor "found," but are actually a complex amalgam of both those dynamics. "Tradition" is not the "things passed on," but the ongoing practice—and indeed, the substantial argument over—the actual process of passing on a faith. Kathryn Tanner has argued something similar in her book *Theories of Culture: A New Agenda for Theology.*

Why do these definitions matter? Because they point to the need to understand that the learning that takes place within theological education has to be about more than "right understanding," or orthodoxy, but also about "right practice," or orthopraxis. Learning takes place in the many ways in which we move and feel our way through learning, just as much as we "think" our way through it. This is a central insight of the recent biological research into memory and meaning-making, even within the field of artificial intelligence—of "robots" such as those who are characters in *A.I.*

As theological educators we care about more than simply transmitting accurate information, although that's important. We also care deeply about finding ways to support our students in living into and living out the traditions we care so much about. One way to talk about this would be to say that we want to be about transformative pedagogies rather than simply transmissive ones; we want to meet the adaptive challenges our communities face, not simply the technical ones.

What might this kind of theological pedagogy look like? There are very many answers, and they are as diverse as the people and contexts within our schools. But here is one example taken from the CD-ROM I mentioned earlier. This is Alejandro Garcia-Rivera:

> [We can do this] by a blurring of the line between where we as theologians, for example, are trained and study, and the place where the pastoral life of the church takes place. . . . I think that what is happening is that there's no longer this place you go to to become educated and then when you come—you come back you're a totally different person, but that, where you learn and what you learn, is also going to be the same place where the life of the church takes place, where people live . . . in our own uniqueness, in our own particularity, somehow we bear the big story, . . . this unique individual also carries the whole story of the universe . . . and then we realize there are no borders, because we carry the big story with us.[8]

How might we carry the Big Story in the midst of digital technologies? To begin with, I think we need to recognize that "digital technologies" are far more than computers on our desktops, useful for e-mail or the Web. While they are certainly that, they are also increasingly the architecture within which mass mediated popular culture is constructed. There is no film, television, radio, magazine, and so on, that is not produced in some way through "bits and bytes." Digital technologies are the warp and woof of our cultural playgrounds. In considering how they carry the Big Story, we would do well to consider what media educators have learned in the past.

The field of media education has shifted dramatically in the last few years, largely because of a shift in the way in which scholars think about how mass media function. It used to be that when thinking about how mass communications technologies "worked," scholars used images such as data pipelines or trucks carrying cargo to talk about how mass media communicated. In these metaphors producers created messages which were then delivered via the mass media, which were essentially large conduits through which the messages flowed. On the other end were the recipients of the messages, who for the most part were passive receivers who "off loaded" the cargo, or took the messages in. Now communications scholars are beginning to talk about mass media as sources of meaning-making materials, as symbolic inventories or cultural databases, of environments from which people draw materials and around which people create rituals that in turn construct meaning. This is another good example of a shift from a "transmissive" or "instrumental" model to one that is "expressive" and oriented to the "reception" of media.

There are two very important consequences of this change in metaphor for media educators. First, the model actually shifts the energy of the meaning-making from the producer of the message to the interaction between the message and those who engage it. We have to understand the diversity of ways in which people make sense of their lives using media, and as media educators who seek to transform such processes, we have to focus on cultural intervention. Growing directly out of this consequence is the second point, which is that while it is still possible to see that mass media have "effects," we have to talk about them in terms of how they shape our practices. Rather than arguing, for instance, that television or film representations of violence "cause" the kinds of violence we saw at Columbine High School, or in other more recent school shootings, media educators ask: What materials were provided as "raw elements" of the meaning-making process around the violence? What kind of attention focus did the media strive to create around these events? What practices did people use to engage the media representations?

Similarly, the researchers who have recently issued reports on the "effects" of media on various communities—possible links between preschool television viewing and later obesity and attentional disorders, for instance, or between television viewing and later violence—do not draw straight-line causal connections between the "viewing" of something and later action on that viewing. Instead, these scholars—like those who are also paying attention to the neuroscience of learning—suggest that it is a pattern of practice that shapes any impact particular media might have on human knowing, human acting. In other words, a household that has five members and one television set will have a very different set of practices with relation to television than will a household of five members and six television sets, and those differences will matter.

You may feel like I've gone down a long tangent here, but religious communities have long been at the heart of experiments with every kind of new media that's appeared. Consider the advent of television. Something about its visual power, or the dawning awareness of its ability to draw mass audiences, sparked enormous effort on the part of religious communities to engage the new medium. There were, roughly speaking, two primary responses. One was a full-scale effort to use it as a tool for evangelization (here you can think about televangelists as being one of the most obvious examples of this mode, or of Cardinal Fulton Sheen's popular show in the 1950s). The other was what might at first appear to be the exact opposite response: a push within many religious communities to develop curricula that taught people how to deconstruct the negative messages of television, how to counter its consumerist values and prescribe gospel values instead.

I say "at first appear," because although these two responses tended to grow out of opposite ends of the theological spectrum—with more conservative communities favoring television as a tool for evangelism and more liberal communities seeking to mitigate its negative "secular" messages—both efforts pretty much assumed that television was a broadband pipeline delivering meaning. In other words, the televangelists decided that it was a pipeline they could use to deliver their own meaning, and media literacy proponents chose to focus their efforts on inoculating people against the negative messages carried through its pipelines.

The one focused on loading its own messages, using it as a tool for its own ends, and the other focused on preventing the "off loading" of negative messages, in some cases even advocating boycotting of various kinds of media. Both understood television primarily, if not entirely, in instrumental terms. What both of these responses missed, however, was the more complicated way in which we engage media, particularly mass media. Some fifty years later, we—that is, people in religious communities who care about media education—have finally begun to realize that it is this underlying conception of how mass media function that has gotten in our way.

Televangelism has ultimately failed to build and nurture strong communities of faith. And the process of trying to inoculate people against negative media messages has instead often inoculated people against *religious* communities, because people have been unwilling to accept such a uniformly negative stance toward a cultural practice they enjoy. So people engaging media—at least those in religious communities—are finally beginning to move beyond either the "it's only a tool to push content" stance or the "we have to inoculate people against it" stance. Instead, media educators are going back to the work of an earlier literacy advocate, Paulo Freire, and struggling to find ways to ensure that we engage mass media with full respect for our own subjectivities. In short, we've begun to work toward an expressive understanding of mass media, one that stresses reception theories.

We are also learning from the biologists who study such things that we have to take seriously the ways in which people engage, resist, contest, and in other ways play with mass media. Media culture—which is increasingly digitally created and mediated—is the water in which all of us swim. It may even be, as Tom Beaudoin argues, the "amniotic fluid" of younger generations.[9] Adán Medrano, a noted filmmaker and videographer, suggests:

> I do think that traditionally we have tended in church circles, the institutional church, to look at media . . . as a visual aid. But rather than just looking at media as a delivery system, the church is now more and more looking at media as the sacramentals of today. . . . These are tactile, media elements, human artifacts that are moments of meeting the divine. These are now media . . . they are popular songs, coming out of MTV . . . [we need to] break the borders of what is sacred and what is profane, and bring into the catechetical forum, into theological forum these media experiences that people are reporting that they have, this is how they are meeting the divine, these are how they are telling the stories, these big mythic stories about good vs. bad struggle, these are in media that people are making, that boundary has been crossed right now. . . .[10]

If we really are going to push for a different understanding of the sacred and profane, or at least recognize that people experience those spaces differently from how we've conceived them in the past, then theological education takes on a particular edge. It pushes us to think about the ways in which we are socialized into various kinds of media practices and seeks to ask foundational questions about our processes of meaning-making. We need to engage people's sense of their lives in daily ways, of which popular media is one. We need to engage media with a clear intent of cultural intervention. We need to understand how we might be crossing borders in the process. So how *can* we engage these digital technologies responsibly and well? How can we practice "the grace of great things" within digital realms?

There are numerous answers to this question which are just now beginning to be experimented with. My own responses grow out of trying to take seriously the expressive nature of media and to fight minimalist and instrumental notions of how digital technologies "work." So how do technology and pedagogy interact in theological education? Through cultural intervention.

Cultural intervention requires that we ask at least the following questions of any medium we choose to engage for the purposes of teaching and learning:

First: *What is the primary grammar or architecture of this medium?* How does it communicate, in what ways do people make meaning within it? Tex Sample argues that our musical "beat" has changed over the last generation and that different music communicates differently.[11] I may not go so far as he, but I do think that electronic screens—whether television or computer monitors—invite us to engage them as windows into a world, and in doing so they shape how we see reality. Fast-paced, moving images, pulsating music, the ability to multitask, to access information quickly—these all shape our knowing and learning in this medium. Before critiquing the limits present, we need to grasp the language. Zull argues that part of our dilemma in shaping learning in such a context is that certain brain "muscles" (metaphorically speaking) have been exercised, while others have been allowed to wither. How do we rebalance, exercise all of the capabilities present for learning?

Second, we must ask what the social infrastructure is that makes it possible to use specific technologies. What kind of an investment does it require of us, both financially as well as socially? Computers exist in such high numbers in the United States at the expense of high consumption of natural resources elsewhere, not to mention significant amounts of cheap labor in other parts of the globe. But they also exist here because of a social infrastructure that has a highly interconnected market system. Globalization—at least in the terms in which Thomas Friedman talks of it—exists only because of the digital infrastructures that make exchange of economic information so seamless and accessible.[12] Pedagogically we need to ask, within graduate theological education, *what patterns of community life are required to maintain pedagogical diversity and freedom in the midst of specific kinds of technologies?*

Third, *in what ways do we want to challenge specific meaning-making frames carried along by specific technologies; how might we stretch a particular technology's abilities enough to recognize its limitations?* How do we build such challenges into the ways in which we use it? If digital technologies make globalization possible, in what other ways might communities of faith understand globalization or stretch and challenge prevailing economic assumptions? What are the practices that we use to make sense within a particular medium, and do those practices make sense for us? And finally, how is God revealing Godself within this medium, and how are we opening ourselves up to that revelation or blinding ourselves to its possibility?

To recap, in integrating digital technologies into theological education, we have to think of our work with them as a process of cultural intervention. We have to be very conscious when we first introduce digital technologies into theological education that many people will primarily think about them in instrumental ways. Do any of these sound familiar? "Computers will make us more efficient." "Computers will bring our courses to a much wider audience." "We have to use computers, they're the future." "Computers will eventually replace teachers." In each of these cases, computers have agency, but we do not, at least not explicitly.

It is not surprising that many faculty are very wary about the process of integrating digital technologies into theological education. We know, deep within ourselves and in our practices, that theological engagement, *logos* about *theos*, is not an instrumental process. It can't be. The Holy Spirit breathes where and how it will, not how we would wish it. If we believe that digital technologies are at heart instrumental, then we are right to resist them. Theological faculty are arbiters, passers on, of a culture, a tradition, and we worry that the cultural imperatives of new technologies will overwhelm us.

When we—that is, people who are trying to bring these technologies to seminaries—treat them primarily as new tools faculty should want to pick up, we risk reinforcing instrumental assumptions at the same time as we ignore the cultural concerns that are legitimately being raised. If we stay within the instrumental framework, we find ourselves forced to argue either that these technologies will allow us to spread the gospel further and more effectively, or admit that we shouldn't use them at all because they recapitulate and reinforce all that we find dangerous about globalization. As with television, both of these positions assumes an instrumental dynamic.

Instead we need to integrate digital technologies into theological pedagogies by understanding that our foundational pedagogies are not instrumental. That is, by understanding how deeply relational and embodied learning is— even when described using the dispassionate language of neuroscience. We need constantly to remind ourselves that learning—and thus the very specific learning that is graduate theological education—is at its heart about practice. We can do this in part by giving people access to digital technologies in ways that deconstruct instrumental assumptions and by encouraging expressive uses of digital technologies.

I mentioned earlier that bringing digital technology into the process at Luther Seminary has sparked much concern and many questions, but that our focus on the missional reasons for doing so created a fruitful context for addressing the concern. I would not be truthful if I didn't acknowledge that "being fruitful" carries some pain. But there are things we've learned—both at Luther and in other contexts I've taught in—that can help to make the process a constructive one, with the pain growing out of giving birth instead of from inducing trauma.

First of all, it's important to understand your institution's pedagogical mission and to be clear about how the goals you have for the integration of technology support that mission. If you don't yet have such a clear vision, then your first steps ought to be to develop a process whereby you can create such a vision. One of my favorite aspects of the now decade-long process of using these technologies within theological education is that it has revitalized questions of teaching and learning.

It may seem counterproductive to spend time debating pedagogical mission when you've got money to be spent on equipment. Or perhaps you've already purchased the equipment, and it's waiting to be used, and now all you want to do is be told how to use it (or tell others how to use it). The temptations to move in instrumental ways are always strong! But I can tell you from experience that if you don't work on raising and responding to these questions now, you will find yourself responding to them later—and probably in more difficult circumstances. Questions suppressed do not go away, they simply become more circuitous and painful. Beyond that, communities of faith remain one of the few spaces left in our culture that are not entirely governed by narratives of profit building, generational isolation, and environmental wreckage. We may well be one of the few cultural spaces left in which some of the ethical questions that surround digital technologies can be raised and engaged. If we stifle the generation of questions—on any issue—we make that kind of inquiry extraordinarily difficult.

What kinds of pedagogical goals might you consider? I would suggest that one place to begin would be with Jack Seymour's typology of theological education.[13] He argues that theological education generally consists of four kinds of activities. Different institutions will emphasize these activities differently, with some neglecting one or more altogether, and others trying to pursue all four to some degree. The four activities in theological education are as follows: theological understanding, denominational socialization, spiritual formation, and the reconstruction of church and society. Can you identify which of these your institution emphasizes? You might want to consider beginning with integrating technology into that component of the curriculum first, and then bringing it to more marginal goals later on.

My second belief grows out of this one: any learning goals you might have need to be arrived at through what Craig Dykstra calls a "process of collaborative inquiry" or "evaluation as purposeful inquiry."[14] He suggests that evaluation, rather than being a process of classification or sorting used for someone else's purposes (such as a funding agent deciding on grants or a teacher who mechanistically assigns letter grades to students), is better understood as a primary principle of reflective practice. I can think of no better way to approach the integration of technology into theological education than to develop a process of collaborative reflective practice around both using such technologies and evaluating their use. Dykstra lists five components of active evaluation pursued in a collaborative way:

1. building into your work regularly scheduled time for reflection on what you are learning;
2. discerning when you want and need the skillful help of others;
3. thinking through as best you can what kind of help you need;
4. finding people you trust to give you what you need in a way that you can use it; and
5. making yourself available and open to receive the help you've asked for.

This is, not incidentally, also a wonderful prescription for active adult learning. The first three are about raising questions, and the next two are about creating conditions that will allow answers to be offered and engaged. Such a process is never easy, and requires learning how to listen. As Jane Hotstream notes:

> It's being able to go beyond your own border. . . . When you cross your own border, that means you're going into a strange territory; in order to do that the biggest challenge is to be able to be centered in a foreign land and not be threatened by everything that looks so foreign and strange. . . . One challenge is to look at yourself and to say what is it that I have to learn in this new area, at this new table so that others can come to the table fully and equally, and there's nothing in me that would block them? And for me then it becomes how do I make adjustments in myself so that others can grow and at the same time I keep growing. That to me is the major journey. And it's the way I talk, it's the way I even sit at the table, when I choose to talk, learning that I don't have all the answers, and that my main job going to this new area is to listen, and listen, and listen, and listen. . . . Any pastoral minister who's not willing to look at themselves and do that in a cultural way, to do that in a way that challenges everything about yourself, everything you think, the way you pray, the way you think about God, the way you relate, if you're not ready to go through that kind of scrutiny, you're not able to minister in a church that is composed of so many different cultural heritages. You can't do it anymore. You can't do it.[15]

To return to where I began, the search for the Blue Fairy, when the young "mecha" David searches for the answer to the question—Can you make me real?—he is presented with an answer by his scientist "father": it is the search, and the desire to pursue that search, that has already made him "real." Yet this is the point of deepest crisis in the film, for in that same scene David discovers that he has been made not unique, but one of many, coming off an assembly line of robot children. He responds by throwing himself off a sky-scraper into the flooded streets of New York City. Neither the fall, nor the submersion, kills him. Instead, he catches a glimpse of the Blue Fairy—enough of a glimpse to renew his search. It is not, finally, the search to be real that has been his goal, but reunion with the source of his relationship, connection with and acknowledgment of his mother's love. The *search* did not define his humanity; rather, *relationality* did. The conclusion to this movie can be "read" in at least two distinctly different ways, but for myself I like to read the final scenes as an ultimate recap of the earliest ones, only this time, instead of it being the mother who yearns for her son, it is the "children"—the mechas who have evolved and survived past their parents—who are yearning for their parents.

In both cases it is the relational bond that is paramount, and in both cases it is a bond that stretches past the purely instrumental. Monica (David's mother) will not accept that this robot is simply a tool for her to use; she refuses to destroy him and instead pushes him out of her home—the catalyst for his journey. Similarly, David can not compel Monica's love, nor even "keep" her past the one day's time that the evolved "mechas" can manage to regenerate her. Instead, it is enough for him that she acknowledges her love for him.

We cannot control God, we cannot even use God for our own ends. Computers will not make that control any more likely. Science cannot make that control more likely. Theologically we know this, and pedagogically we need to accept it as well. It is our questions that can open us up to new relationships, and it is our questions that, when grounded in community and humility—in the "grace of great things"—can nurture our faith.

Roberto Goizueta believes there are crucial questions arising out of our faith right now:

> . . . what is the role of popular religion, the way in which people actually live out their Christian faith, especially the Latino community, and how do these rituals, stories, symbols, devotions, how do they reveal God to us? Not just to us, but to the church as a whole? . . . How do we understand ourselves, and how does . . . globalization, how does that intercultural reality affect how we understand our God?[16]

How do we understand our God? And are we faith-filled enough to imagine a way in which God could be revealing Godself in the midst of our search to integrate digital technologies into theological education? These are the kinds of questions I think we need to put at the heart of our process and that make powerful goals for teaching within graduate theological education.

FOR FURTHER REFLECTION

Films

Galaxy Quest. DVD. Directed by Dean Parisot. Universal/MCA, 2003.
The Matrix. DVD. Directed by Larry Wachowski and Andy Wachowski. Warner Studios, 1999.
Pleasantville. DVD. Directed by Gary Ross. New Line Home Video, 1999.
The Truman Show. DVD. Directed by Peter Weir. Paramount Studio, 2003.

QUESTIONS FOR FACULTY DISCUSSION

What are the primary goals of your institution?
What are the reasons you're contemplating using digital technologies?
What is the context in which you're working?
What are the fears that these technologies raise for you?
Where in Seymour's typology does your institution invest most of its energy? Where do you?
Where are there resources for collaborative inquiry in your institution?

NOTES

1. *A.I.* DVD. Directed by Steven Spielberg. Universal Studios, 2001.
2. Margaret Miles, *Seeing and Believing: Religion and Values in the Movies* (Boston: Beacon Press, 1996), 25.
3. Mary Boys, *Educating in Faith: Maps and Visions* (San Francisco: Harper and Row, 1989).
4. *Beyond Borders: Ministry in the Multicultural World.* CD-ROM (JMCommunications.com, 2002). This CD-ROM can be ordered online through the Mexican American Cultural Center (www.maccsa.org/).
5. *Beyond Borders*, interview with Dr. Gloria Lloyd.
6. James Zull, *The Art of Changing the Brain: Enriching Teaching by Exploring the Biology of Learning* (Sterling, VA: Stylus Publishing, 2002), 245.
7. Zull, *Changing the Brain,* 159.
8. *Beyond Borders,* interview with Dr. Alejandro Garcia-Rivera.
9. Thomas Beaudoin, *Virtual Faith: The Irreverent Spiritual Quest of Generation X* (San Francisco: Jossey-Bass, 1998).
10. *Beyond Borders,* interview with Adán Medrano.
11. Tex Sample, *The Spectacle of Worship in a Wired World: Electronic Culture and the Gathered People of God* (Nashville, TN: Abingdon Press, 1998).
12. Thomas Friedman, *The Lexus and the Olive Tree* (New York: Anchor Books, 2000).

13. Jack Seymour, "Approaches to Theological Education" (lecture, Wabash Center summer workshop, Wabash College, Crawfordsville, IN, 1999).

14. Craig Dykstra, "Evaluation as Collaborative Inquiry," in *Initiatives in Religion: A Newsletter of Lilly Endowment, Inc.* 2, no. 4 (fall 1993). Available online at www.resourcingchristianity.org/Newsletter.aspx?ID=1.

15. *Beyond Borders,* interview with Dr. Jane Hotstream.

16. *Beyond Borders,* interview with Dr. Roberto Goizueta.

Chapter Three

Understanding by Design: Creating Learning Experiences That Meet the Challenges of the Twenty-first Century

The September 10, 2001, issue of *America* reported that "there are more than 300 professional Catholic lay ministry formation programs in the United States, with a combined enrollment of more than 35,000—about 10 times the number of seminarians in post-college studies and 13 times the number of men in deacon formation programs."[1] Around the same time I read that article, I was part of a forum at Luther Seminary in St. Paul, Minnesota, in which one participant noted that "as many people are entering public leadership in the ELCA through nonseminary, nonjuridical routes, as are entering each year from all eight ELCA seminaries combined."[2] This latter statement is more anecdotal than statistically verifiable, but it still highlights a similar trend to the one occurring in Catholic contexts.

Why do these observations matter in reflecting upon digital technologies in theological education? In part because they point to the reality that more and more of the people entering pastoral leadership in our churches these days do not come through the "traditional" routes people have used in the past. But they also matter because our seminaries and graduate theological programs are embedded in contexts in which there are multiple paths toward pastoral leadership, multiple ways to prepare for such service, and multiple reasons to do so. One of the primary ways in which seminaries have been using digital technologies is to implement "distributive education"—or programs of study implemented using the Internet to transcend time and/or geographic limitations. Digital technologies can certainly be extraordinarily useful in expanding access to our learning programs, but only if we implement them in ways that follow from our goals, not that drive them.

One way to ensure that our teaching/learning practices are thoroughly embedded in our shared goals is by designing our courses in that way. McTighe and Wiggins are two scholars of curriculum development who speak to this issue in ways that are particularly compelling for those of us within theological education. They have written of curriculum design as being a process of supporting understanding, with a notion of what constitutes "understanding" that is rich and complex. Their rubric for the "six facets of understanding" provides a guide for assessing our teaching practices in multiple and complex ways (see fig. 3.1).

As is clear in this chart, saying "I understand that" means far more than simply "I can explain that."[3] The Wiggins/McTighe rubric suggests that there are six elements to understanding: explanation, interpretation, application, perspective, empathy, and self-knowledge. The first three—the ability to explain, interpret, and apply something—are familiar to educators. Most of us can identify various levels of such ability and can point to ways in which our own teaching is directed at helping students to develop one or more of these three elements of understanding. But the latter three—perspective, empathy, and self-knowledge—are not as familiar, even though they are at the heart of any commitment to ensuring that theological education is a "relational, embodied" enterprise.

In 2003 Sheryl Crow released a wildly popular song, initially through an exclusive arrangement with Apple Computer's iTunes store. The refrain from that song—"you gotta believe in what you feel, and feel what you believe"— was popular in part because of its catchy tune and danceable rhythm, but also in part because belief and feeling are so intimately wound together in our contemporary context. The "postmodern" context we inhabit, a context in which there is widespread rejection of claims to absolute knowledge, a context in which we engage most institutions with significant skepticism and concern about the ways in which languages of "power over" permeate our social and political spaces, and a context in which we greet "difference" with more openness and even celebration than was once the case,[4] is also a context in which feeling and belief are so tightly commingled as to be difficult to separate. The Wiggins/McTighe rubric provides one entry point into acknowledging this context and also suggests ways to assess students' development within it.

One reason the rubric is so important is precisely for this ability to assess a spectrum of learning. Most teachers can trace ways in which students' ability to explain something can span the gamut from naïve to sophisticated, or their ability to interpret something might run from literal to profound. But it has been much more difficult to name, let alone teach toward, a spectrum of self-understanding. The point of any rubric is not to "judge" people and find them wanting, but rather to identify where someone is in their learning journey so as to support them in the next steps. In the context of theological education—or even religious education more broadly construed—we (as teachers) want our students to be able to move from more narrow and self-bound understanding to more open and empathetic positions. How to do so? Wiggins and McTighe suggest that we must work "backwards" in designing for understanding. Rather than starting from a huge database of the content we hope to convey and then figuring out ways to transfer that content, they argue that we must first ask what the learning goal is; next, what evidence will demonstrate that a student has achieved that goal; and then only at that point determine a learning task that will support the student in developing sufficient skill to provide such evidence.

This kind of framework works from the most narrowly defined technical information to the most broadly construed creative goal. Consider the teaching of Greek, generally a fairly discrete, technical process. What goal do most seminaries have in relation to acquiring Greek? In ours, at least, the goal is that students become comfortable enough reading koine Greek to read in their original language the texts they will be preaching upon and teaching in congregational settings. That goal, in turn, is based on our belief that in order to be both respectful and creative interpreters, students need to engage these texts in their original languages. Here we want our students to be able to *understand* the text, not simply parse its grammar. We invite them *into* the world of the text, and in doing so invite them *out* of their own limited experiences. This is surely an invitation to deeper empathy, perspective, and self-knowledge. In teaching toward this goal, our faculty teach the language using texts that are similar, if not identical, to the texts that students will encounter in their later contexts. How one translates a particular prepositional phrase has consequences for the meaning of the phrase, and those implications, in turn, draw our students more deeply into the practice of translation and interpretation.

Yet inviting students into such a deep practice of understanding is not an easy task, and it can be very difficult to sustain the connections between the difficult, patient task of learning Greek words and discerning the theological implications of specific choices—let alone how those choices impact one's preaching. In a context in which believing and feeling are so intertwined, how to help students "feel" their way into Greek?

To answer that question, I need to take a few steps back and lay out some basic principles of learning design. Every semester, for instance, as I teach my introductory course in Christian education, we begin with what I call a "trio of triads." These groups of three concepts from the educational literatures follow us through the term and allow us to consider a whole host of issues in Christian faith nurture from a common yet flexible perspective. Here, too, they are useful for charting a course through the bumpy waters of the post-modern excursion. The first triad I work with is very basic: any learning event

Explanation	Interpretation	Application
Sophisticated: an unusually thorough, elegant, and inventive account (model, theory, or explanation); fully supported, verified, and justified; deep and broad: goes well beyond the information given.	*Profound:* a powerful and illuminating interpretation and analysis of the importance/meaning/ significance; tells a rich and insightful story; provides a rich history or context; sees deeply and incisively any ironies in the different interpretations.	*Masterful:* fluent, flexible, and efficient; able to use knowledge and skill and adjust understandings well in novel, diverse, and difficult contexts.
In-depth: an atypical and revealing account, going beyond what was explicitly taught; makes subtle connections; well supported by argument and evidence; novel thinking displayed.	*Revealing:* a nuanced interpretation and analysis of the importance/meaning/ significance; tells an insightful story; provides a telling history or context; sees subtle differences, levels, and ironies in diverse interpretations.	*Skilled:* competent in using knowledge and skill and adapting understandings in a variety of appropriate and demanding contexts.
Developed: an account that reflects some in-depth and personalized ideas; the student is making the work her own, going beyond the given—there is supported theory here, but insufficient or inadequate evidence and argument.	*Perceptive:* a helpful interpretation or analysis of the importance/meaning/ significance; tells a clear and instructive story; provides a useful history or context; sees different levels of interpretation.	*Able:* able to perform well with knowledge and skill in a few contexts, with a limited repertoire, flexibility, or adaptability to diverse contexts.
Intuitive: an incomplete account but with apt and insightful ideas; extends and deepens some of what was learned; some "reading between the lines"; account has limited support/argument/data or sweeping generalizations. There is a theory, but one with limited testing and evidence.	*Interpreted:* a plausible interpretation or analysis of the importance/meaning/ significance; makes sense of a story; provides a history or context.	*Apprentice:* relies on a limited repertoire of routines; able to perform well in familiar or simple contexts, with perhaps some needed coaching; limited use of personal judgment and responiveness to specifics of feedback/situation.
Naïve: a superficial account; more descriptive than analytical or creative; a fragmentary or sketchy account of facts/ideas or glib generalizations; a black-and-white account; less a theory than an unexamined hunch or borrowed idea.	*Literal:* a simplistic or superficial reading; mechanical translation; a decoding with little or no sense of wider importance or significance; a restatement of what was taught or read.	*Novice:* can perform only with coaching or relies on highly scripted, singular "plug-in" (algorithmic and mechanical) skills, procedures, or approaches.

Figure 3.1   Rubric for the Six Facets of Understanding

Perspective	Empathy	Self-Knowledge
Insightful: a penetrating and novel viewpoint; effectively critiques and encompasses other plausible perspectives; takes a long and dispassionate, critical view of the issues involved.	*Mature:* disposed and able to see and feel what others see and feel; usually open to and willing to seek out the odd, alien, or different.	*Wise:* deeply aware of the boundaries of one's own and others' understanding; able to recognize his prejudices and projections; has integrity— able and willing to act on what one understands.
Thorough: a revealing and coordinated critcal view; makes own view more plausible by considering the plausiblity of other perspectives; makes apt criticisms, discriminations, and qualifications.	*Sensitive:* disposed to see and feel what others see and feel; open to the unfamiliar or different.	*Circumspect:* aware of one's ignorance and that of others; aware of one's prejudices; knows the strengths and limits of one's understanding.
Considered: a reasonably critical and comprehensive look at all points of view in the context of one's own; makes clear that there is plausibility to other points of view.	*Aware:* knows and feels that others see and feel differently; somewhat able to empathize with others; has difficulty making sense of odd or alien views.	*Thoughtful:* generally aware of what is and is not understood; aware of how prejudice and projection can occur without awareness and shape one's views.
Aware: knows of different points of view and somewhat able to place own view in perspective, but weakness in considering worth of each perspective or critiquing each perspective, especially one's own; uncritial about tacit assumptions.	*Developing:* has aome capacity and self-discipline to "walk in another's shoes," but is still primarily limited to one's own reactions and attitudes; puzzled or put off by different feelings or attitudes.	*Unreflective:* generally unaware of one's specific ignorance; generally unaware of how subjective prejudgments color understandings.
Uncritical: unaware of differing points of view; prone to overlook or ignore other perspectives; has difficulty imagining other ways of seeing things; prone to egocentric argument and personal criticisms.	*Egocentric:* has little or no empathy beyond intellectual awareness of others; sees things through own ideas and feelings; ignores or is threatened or puzzled by different feelings, attitudes, or views.	*Innocent:* completely unaware of the bounds of one's understanding and of the role of projection and prejudice in opinions and attempts to understand.

always rests on three elements—the people involved, the purpose for which they have gathered, and the context in which the learning is taking place (people, purpose, context).

The statistics with which I began this chapter suggest that at least one of these elements has shifted dramatically in the last few decades—the context in which graduate theological education takes place. People entering public religious leadership are no longer streaming through the doors of traditional seminaries. Preparation for this kind of religious leadership (that is, non-ordained leadership) is increasingly taking place in contexts that are only loosely linked, if at all, to traditional institutions of theological education. Churches are "growing" youth leaders within their midst, utilizing the expertise of their congregants trained for other institutions (such as businesses and nonprofit organizations), or identifying very specialized forms of ministry (such as music ministry) that draw people from "secular" institutions.

There are many reasons behind this shift, but one of the most obvious is linked to a second element of this triad—people. Most seminaries were established to serve the needs of people preparing for ordained ministry at a time when people came to a sense of their call early in their lives. Most such students knew by the time they left college, if not high school, that they wanted to prepare to enter ordained ministry. They were most often young, male, and able to participate in a process of ministerial education that involved long stretches of residence on a campus interspersed with periods of intense practicum in a local parish. Seminary education was built around the needs of such students, and to some lingering extent it still is. Yet the majority of students responding to a call to ordained leadership today no longer fit this description. The Association of Theological Schools (ATS) *Fact Book on Theological Education* notes that across all ATS schools, "more than fifty percent (51.95%) of the total head count enrollment was 35 years or older . . . " Women now account for 34.91% of the total enrollment across ATS schools, even though they are precluded from participating in some programs. At Luther Seminary our classes are now roughly 50/50 in terms of gender.[5]

With this shift in both the people who are entering theological education and the immediate context in which it is taking place comes the third element of my triad—purpose. The reasons for which students enter graduate theological education no longer carry the uniformity of purpose that "becoming a pastor" once implied. Certainly many, many students enter seminary with precisely that goal in mind. But many others are preparing for other kinds of ministries or are at the beginning of a longer faith journey in which seminary is simply the first step in deepening their spiritual awareness and religious commitments.

People, purpose, context: in introducing this triad, I used the notion of "context" very simply, but, as with any of these terms, there are both broad and deep elements contained within it. "Context" is a word that is increasingly in use in theological education, but often with more than one meaning. At its root, the word has to do with "the interrelated conditions in which something exists or occurs."[6] We may speak of "contextual education" when we think about the parts of a seminary degree that require a student to work within a parish setting for a year before graduating. Yet we also talk about "reading the context" in various kinds of theologies, particularly those that have feminist or liberationist roots. I use the word "context" in some ways to parallel closely another oft-used word, "culture."

"Culture" can be defined as all those activities that allow someone to give meaning to, draw meaning from, and derive meaning within a specific location. When we consider the shifts that are underway in graduate theological education at the moment, we have to take into account the ways in which the larger contexts in which our institutions are embedded are shifting, and here the word "culture" is particularly helpful. It is not just our student body that has changed; it is also the myriad cultural contexts surrounding and permeating our institutions that have changed.

As mentioned earlier, I teach at a large Lutheran (ELCA) institution in the upper Midwest, although I am myself a Roman Catholic layperson. Even two decades ago it was possible for students and faculty at this institution to rely on the culture surrounding the seminary to prepare students for entrance into theological study. "Christendom" might be a term that is no longer in much use, but just twenty years ago it was perhaps still descriptive of a certain kind of Lutheran reality in the northern reaches of the midwestern United States. We could count on our entering students to be familiar with the Christian Bible, to have an understanding of their identity as Lutherans, and to be comfortable with basic worship practices. Our task as a seminary was to help them deepen and reflect critically upon these understandings and commitments.

Now we find ourselves at a different starting point. Many of our students have little if any familiarity with scripture texts, Lutheran confessions, or the rhythms of Lutheran worship. In part this is because some of them are not Lutheran, but in part it is also because those who are Lutheran were not deeply immersed in Christian education as children and may have come with college degrees in apparently unrelated fields (accounting, physical education, and so on).

Even this degree of unfamiliarity would not pose the kind of challenge we are facing if it was accompanied by thorough grounding in religious culture, ease of use and fluency with print discourses, and an ability to self-consciously reflect upon personal experience. Instead we have students who come to us fluent in digital technologies, with ritual experiences shaped by television and film, and with reflective patterns shaped more by sympathetic identification than philosophical argument.[7] Can you begin to see how "people, purpose, and context" come together, and how influential they are within educational contexts? Certainly our earliest Christian educational leadership—such as Paul's correspondence to the scattered churches— demonstrates an exquisite sensitivity to context and to the purposes for which one gathers in Christian community.

If learning experiences are fundamentally shaped by people, purpose, and context, then seminary educators need to take note of the dramatic changes occurring in our midst. Many of us, trained in the rigorous print-based searches of scholarly pursuit, are uncomfortable with these changes and are more challenged than affirmed by them. We worry about the coherence of the thought taking place around us, we struggle to tend our own disciplines at the same time as we ponder how to make them relevant to students who have no interest in scholarly endeavors, and we sometimes fall into the quagmire of assuming our own experiences—particularly in worship—are normative.

So what are we to do? If considering the triad of "people, purpose, and context" brings us these challenges, perhaps the next triad—cognitive, affective, and psychomotor—can help us to address them. This triad utilizes terms that are drawn primarily from the psychological disciplines. For my students I sometimes begin by suggesting that a simpler version—ideas, feelings, and actions—might make more sense. The key to this triad, however, lies in the recognition that learning always takes place in multiple ways. In any given learning environment we might be intentionally focusing on one of these processes, but the other two are involved as well.

During the time when seminary education took place within a more homogenous cultural context and seminary students shared more in common than their differences, teachers did not have to attend quite so carefully to this tripartite learning model. Feelings and actions—the affective and the psychomotor— were a language that shared similar terms and that were built into shared assumptions. A male teacher putting a friendly arm around the shoulder of a young male student in the context of exploring the unease generated by a historical-critical approach to a biblical text could be "read" as supporting that student's struggle and encouraging the student's pursuit of truth. In our current context, the same action could be read quite differently—and in multiple ways. Nonverbal gestural sign systems, what many of us call "body language," differ amongst genders and between cultural locations. Now we must be more aware of them, more intentionally reflective of how we engage them, and more thoughtful of their multiple interpretations.

Rather than being another problem, however, this is an enormous opportunity. The wider cultural contexts we inhabit, particularly those of the digitally mediated, globalized village that is increasingly the United States, are contexts in which nonverbal gestural sign systems are in a rich and abundant array of usage. As Medrano and others have argued, we approach digital media in ways more akin to ritual practice than print-oriented practice.[8] This suggests that the kinds of traditions we represent, the meaning-making databases we tend, if you will, have never been more necessary than they are now. It also opens up vast new arenas for scholarly pursuit of fundamentally important questions. Finally, it provides a framework in which we can approach the students who enter our contexts with a greater degree of respect and openness, because we can be intentionally thoughtful about all of the levels on which their learning is occurring.

There is one final triad in my set of trios, which is a group that Elliott Eisner first identified—the "explicit, the implicit, and the null curriculum."[9] Here, again, I sometimes simplify these terms for my students, talking instead about those things we "intentionally" seek to teach, those things students learn "incidentally," and the things we teach and students learn because we do not address them directly, what some have called "unacknowledged" learning.

When combined with the previous triad, this group is particularly helpful in identifying some of the opportunities present in the challenges we face in graduate theological education in our current contexts. Consider, for instance, the ways in which students may be highly adept at "sympathetic identification" through their socialization into media culture but quite unfamiliar with basic philosophical argumentation. A teacher who begins a course by expecting students to do brief philosophical essays as a way to demonstrate their grasp of liturgical theology may find herself with a line of students outside her door complaining about the irrelevance of such an assignment.

The teacher intentionally designed an assignment to support students' critical reflection on a crucial element of any pastor's practice. The students, however, span the gamut from those who are planning on being pastors to those who are simply fulfilling a requirement of the curriculum on their way to doctoral studies. For the first group, the assignment strikes them on the implicit or incidental level as a "misread" of their needs in the course, and if their emotions are engaged in opposition to the teacher, it becomes a serious problem to support their learning much of anything in that context. For the second group, brief essays may seem like a trivial hoop to jump through rather than a space in which to explore important theological issues. For both groups the "feeling" level of the assignment sends an incidental message that the teacher does not respect them and does not understand their context. They may be spurred to any number of actions, amongst which could be disengagement from the course in all but the most passive mode, or outright hostility.

On the other hand, a teacher could design the early part of a worship course with sufficient attention to the embodied nature of liturgy—perhaps requiring students to experience multiple forms of worship in various churches or asking them to be "visitors" in another tradition—and then require students to engage those experiences in a descriptive essay first, a more critical essay next, and finally a philosophical essay that uses concepts drawn from liturgical theology to explore their experiences. In this case, the student is being supported by first being invited into an experience, next being asked to describe it in narrative form, after that being asked to reflect upon it more deeply, and finally going back to that experience with a full complement of theological terms to draw upon in interrogating it.

I can already hear the concerns my colleagues might raise: if we do all of that, how can we possibly accomplish all that we need to in a course? Isn't it important to challenge students and require them to live up to expectations rather than to "dumb down" our approaches? How can we possibly design such assignments to meet the diverse needs of all of our students?

Let me take each of these objections in turn. First, the concern about coverage of material. There is significant research from the last decade that suggests that students learn more when presented with less. That might seem counterintuitive, but consider the ways in which scholarly work often proceeds: A question begins to occur to you, and you ask yourself what your response to it might be. If no answer emerges, your next response might be to ask a friend or colleague what their "take" on it would be, or you might go to a presentation at a conference or look for an article that deals with the general topic. It is only after fussing around with it for a while that you begin to refine your questions, and then, and probably only then, will you be able to turn to more focused and philosophical texts to help you structure your response.

It is almost a truism of adult education now that adult learners need to be supported into self-initiating inquiry. Another way to think about this would be to use Parker Palmer's description of the "grace of great things." His argument is that we teach more by going deeply, even if narrowly, than we do by going broadly but staying near the surface.[10] Our students live in an information-rich, even information-saturated, environment. It is far more important for us to help them develop information-accessing abilities, information-critiquing abilities, and information-integrating abilities than it is that we transfer content to them. So, as one of my friends often puts it, we need "just in time" learning rather than "just in case" learning.

The second objection a colleague might raise is the concern about challenging students rather than lowering content standards. This is an important objection, because educational scholarship also points repeatedly to the necessity of asking students to reach up rather than not requiring enough of them. The key, here, however, is linked to the triad of "ideas, feelings, and actions" along with the "explicit, implicit, and null." Far too often we make extraordinarily challenging assignments without recognizing how hard they are, let alone providing sufficient support to meet their challenges.

A case in point: We, as scholars and representatives of historically grounded religious communities, often have personal histories of deep and prolonged experiences of religious community that are complex, diverse in character, and richly meaningful. We come to teach theological disciplines with these experiences in our background and often teach with the assumption that our students will trust our knowledge and experience enough to accept our guidance as to what they need to know and how to go about learning it. Our students, on the other hand, often come from quite impoverished experiences of religious community, perhaps having only one, or at best two or three, kinds of worship to draw upon, or having only encountered one form of biblical interpretation. Many of our students find various other kinds of spiritual engagement—attending a film with friends, engaging in sporting events, activism—at least as, if not more, profoundly engaging than activities associated with religious institutions.[11] They praise God and reconcile themselves with God in a range of ways we may only dimly fathom and for which we may have little respect.

Thus they enter our classrooms with some distrust, if not open suspicion, of the ability of a professor in an academic institution to speak to their experiences with any knowledge or utility. When we teach from our background experiences and assume that they are shared, we are already sending, on an implicit level, the wrong messages. If we then refuse to engage our students' questions—particularly those that have to do with media culture, or various forms of music (both of which are issues of deep and constitutive importance to many of them)—we teach through the "null" curriculum that we do not respect these experiences and consequently do not respect our students. It is thus a deeply challenging assignment we make to our students—to come into our classrooms and meet us more than halfway; to submerge their own experiences, intuitions, and instincts, to submerge the better part of their experiential resonances, and in turn to accept our claims and definitions as binding.

That is an extraordinarily challenging task and teaches a number of lessons that I believe we do not want to teach. On the other hand, if we can invite our students' experiences into our classrooms with sufficient hospitality and respect, we may be able to develop a shared language that could support them in coming to a deeper recognition of the shared riches of religious traditions and the necessity of evaluating our emotional or experiential resonances against the hew and grain of our traditions. My argument here is that we, as teachers, need to be aware of the "clay" with which we are encasing the riches of the tradition. We must also be aware of the treasures our students may be unearthing, if we could only collaborate with them.

The third objection my hypothetical colleague might raise grows out of a deep concern for teaching in ways that have coherence and respect for students. How can we, indeed, teach in such a way as to meet the needs of all the diverse students in our classrooms? There is no simple answer to this question, and it is an important issue. It is our task as teachers to provide coherence and substance for our students and to respect them in their diversity. These two goals can be in conflict. The tension between the two can be so strong that we may retreat into a standardized curriculum that does not fit anyone well but at least has the virtue of being standardized. Or the tension can lead us to be "good enough" teachers, putting together materials that meet the needs of most of the students, most of the time. This has been the position I have tried to take in my own teaching. But ultimately there is also what Palmer calls the "grace of great things" to take into account. He argues that:

> We invite *diversity* into our community not because it is politically correct but because diverse viewpoints are demanded by the manifold mysteries of great things. We embrace *ambiguity* not because we are confused or indecisive but because we understand the inadequacy of our concepts to embrace the vastness of great things. We welcome *creative conflict* not because we are angry or hostile but because conflict is required to correct our biases and prejudices about the nature of great things. We practice *honesty* not only because we owe it to one another but because to lie about what we have seen would be to betray the truth of great things. We experience *humility* not because we have fought and lost but because humility is the only lens through which great things can be seen—and once we have seen them, humility is the only posture possible. We become *free* men and women through education not because we have privileged information but because tyranny in any form can be overcome only by invoking the grace of great things.[12]

One of the benefits of focusing on the "grace of great things" and the practices that go along with it is that it can free us as teachers to experience the humility of being in the presence of God. I am not the primary teacher in any learning environment, the Holy Spirit is.

Toward that end I work to develop frameworks for learning events that are as flexible and choice driven as possible. In the beginning of any class, for instance, requiring students to develop their own learning goals in relation to the stated goals of a course helps to alert me to ways in which the design of the course needs to be modified or to individual students who might need extra support. Developing a syllabus that has a menu of assignment options can be one element of such flexibility, giving students the ability to choose assignments that match their intelligences and their learning styles, not to mention their diverse purposes in coming to seminary. Asking students to fill out brief half sheets after a lecture, in which they must list one thing they have learned and one thing about which they still have questions, can make even highly scripted lectures an interactive process over time. Using critical incident inquiry reports, with the teacher reporting back to the class what they (teacher and student alike) are learning, conveys respect and nurtures deeper engagement. These kinds of choices can themselves increase the difficulty of a course, because many students have been socialized into being passive learners. Yet the earlier they can be supported into taking charge of their own learning, the earlier it is possible to effect convergence along all the curricula (explicit, implicit, null).

To return to my earlier example from the Greek language class, there are multiple methods that could be employed to provide opportunities to learn across the many layers of the rubric. Helping students develop small learning groups in which to practice the specific skills, using familiar texts to provide context for grammar issues, inviting students into pressing contemporary theological problems that can be interpreted differently depending on the underlying Greek translation, and so on, are all examples that many teachers have already embedded in their classes.

A trio of triads: (1) people, purpose, context; (2) cognitive, affective, psychomotor; (3) explicit, implicit, null curricula. Each of these lenses has helped to point to some of the challenges we face in Christian higher education. But these are, in some ways, only a lens through which to name the difficulties. There are two profound challenges facing Christian higher education that we have only briefly skated across, and it is to these challenges that I will turn for the rest of this chapter.

THINKING THROUGH OTHERS

The first of the two challenges has to do with the ways in which we are essentially working "across cultures" in our teaching and learning. There are many ways to speak of this challenge—and many have done so. In this essay I will speak to only one such cross-cultural work—that of the print-based academy and the mass mediated popular culture context outside of it. I have written in earlier chapters about this divide, but let me turn now to a useful framework for engaging, that of R. Shweder's "thinking through others."

Shweder, a cultural anthropologist, has developed a four-part typology for the ways in which anthropologists "think through others." His framework suggests that they do so by thinking by means of the other, getting the other straight, deconstructing and going beyond the other, and witnessing in the context of engagement with the other. Each of these strategies follows in succession, and so it is worth taking them each in turn. "Thinking by means of the other" has to do with engaging some aspect of the "other" as a means to learn more about ourselves:

> "Thinking through others" in the first sense is to recognize the other as a specialist or expert on some aspect of human experience, whose reflective consciousness and systems of representations and discourse can be used to reveal hidden dimensions of our selves.[13]

This first mode requires an honest acknowledgment of the ways in which the "other"—here I am suggesting academic culture and mass mediated popular culture as "other" in relation—can indeed be expert in some way.

Faculty at graduate theological institutions are familiar with thinking of ourselves as "experts" in various kinds of discourse and study that can reveal hidden dimensions of thought and reality. But how often do we acknowledge that media culture might also hold resources to bring to this task? Certainly our students are expected to recognize and grant authority to our expertise, but how often do we acknowledge our students' fluency in the discourses of popular culture? There are rare professors who hire students to write Web pages for them, for instance, or to serve as participant observers in ethnographic observations of youth culture. But even here, we, the faculty, hold the defining and controlling expertise. Yet it is out in media culture that the most relevant questions of faith are being debated—this is perhaps nowhere more clear than in the public debates over the Iraq war, or the interpretations of Mel Gibson's film *The Passion of the Christ*. It is within digital media (a category which includes television, film, radio, and the World Wide Web, among others) that decisions are being made on questions of crucial communal importance.

Shweder's second mode is something he terms "getting the other straight," by which he means "providing a systematic account of the internal logic of the intentional world constructed by the other. The aim is a rational reconstruction of indigenous belief, desire, and practice."[14] This mode of inquiry has so much in common with historical-critical biblical practice as to require little explanation here. Yet it is precisely that commonality—and the tendency of using those tools in isolation and thus sending the implicit message of "otherness"—that is most challenging to many of our students, since the "conclusion" they draw from using historical-critical tools can be that the Bible is a thought-world so different from ours as to be accessible only through specialized tools. This same message is often sent, again unintentionally, by Bible studies structured in small groups of lay people circled around an expert pastor who holds forth on the correct interpretation of a text.

Another example might be the way that we seek in teaching worship to provide a "systematic account of the intentional world constructed"; not, in this case, by "the other," but rather by us, in community. Media studies scholars have shifted their understanding of how mass media operate over the last two decades from a model that might be called "instrumental" to one that is far more open to the expressive reception of media. No longer are media producers viewed as solely determining the meaning of any "texts" channeled through digital media, but rather are seen as only one partner in a complicated dance of meaning-creation. One analogy these scholars have used for describing the ways in which we engage media is that of "ritual." In that analogy, people engage digital media as a resource in meaning-making; we use a set of practices that seek to shape time and location in engaging various digital media. We can "get lost," for instance, on the Web, emerging hours later with no sense of time passing. We listen to a background version of the radio, seeking to hear other people make sense of the day's events while we make dinner or finish our commute.

How often do worship faculty ask students to think about the ritual implications of their media practices? This is an important question, and perhaps no more so than now, when worship faculty are increasingly being asked to reflect upon the use of digital media within worship. In what ways do our students' socialization within media culture shape the discourses and patterns of practice we seek to facilitate within worship? It is just as important for us to be able to give a "systematic account of the intentional world constructed" by digital media, as it is for our students to be able to do so of the world we seek to name and proclaim through worship.

Shweder's third mode, at least from the point of view of anthropology, involves "going beyond the other." Many educators would identify this mode as "critical reflection," and indeed that mode shares a lot in common with Shweder's description:

> It is a third sense, for it properly comes later, after we have already appreciated what the intentional world of the other powerfully reveals and illuminates, from its special point of view. "Thinking through others" is, in its totality, an act of criticism and liberation, as well as discovery.[15]

It is this third mode that I believe we as teachers are most anxious to support our students in "getting." It is an ability that falls on the more sophisticated end of the understanding rubric for perspective, for empathy, for self-knowledge. Yet it is Shweder's assertion—and mine as well—that this is properly achieved only after first moving through "thinking by means of the other" and "getting the other straight." Earlier in this chapter I pointed to some of the problems that can occur when teachers ignore the affective and psychomotor components of learning, or when we refuse to consider the implicit or null curricula embedded in our teaching. These are the same dilemmas that emerge when teachers move too quickly to "go beyond others." We face an enormous opportunity in the middle of the postmodern context if we can bring our analytical and creative minds to bear on the issues that appear before us, on the questions that our students bring to us. But that opportunity contains within it an enormous abyss of difficulty if we move too quickly to critique digital media, for instance, without first considering them from within their own framework. We can invite our students into shared ritual leadership, or we can refuse to respect their own learning and contexts and simply try to transfer to them our own understandings. The latter stance will drive more people out of the church than it will invite in.

Yet there is an important step here, as Shweder acknowledges, a step that can be deeply respectful, of moving to think beyond digital culture. This same step requires us to think beyond and through institutional religious culture. Sociologists point to the deep skepticism members of the GenX community have toward institutions. Often that skepticism is expressed primarily toward religious institutions rather than media institutions. Perhaps we could respectfully invite young leaders within GenX and millennial spaces into religious institutions, thus in some ways bringing their criticism "inside" while at the same time encouraging them to turn their critical lenses onto media institutions.

Shweder's fourth mode is "witnessing in the context of engagement with the other":

> In this fourth sense of "thinking through others," the process of representing the other goes hand in hand with a process of portraying one's own self as part of the process of representing the other, thereby encouraging an open-ended self-reflexive dialogic turn of mind.[16]

This last mode of engaging the "other" is the mode with which we have the least experience in religious institutions. Far too often we engage in conversations across differences — whether ecumenically or in interfaith dialogue — from the arrogant position of having the truth rather than from the humble position of confessing that the Holy Spirit is ever at work in the world, continuing to reveal God to us. Again, if the years since September 11, 2001, have taught us anything, I would hope that we have begun to learn that supporting rigid or fundamental religious identity formation can have the effect of creating an environment in which terrorism can flourish rather than of bringing us to our knees in awe at all that God has created among us.

Perhaps the clearest example of the way in which we as theological educators "witness in the context of engagement with the other" can be found in the ways in which we as teachers embody the deep humility of the teacher who is drawn to teaching because she is drawn to learning. As much as Martin Luther fought to keep hold of critical reason in relation to scripture, it was also he who helped to liberate scripture from the tyranny of an elite educated class of interpreters. Bible studies that are open circles of inquiry, shaped by the evaluative criteria of a historically grounded tradition but open to the emerging questions and life experiences of contemporary readers, exemplify this "open-ended, self-reflexive dialogic turn of mind."

THE END OF EDUCATION

The final challenge I find deeply embedded in the examples I used at the beginning of this chapter is the third leg of the first triad—that of purpose. What is the "end" of graduate theological education? Up until 1994 Luther Seminary's mission statement read:

> Luther Northwestern educates men and women to serve the mission of the gospel of Jesus Christ. Congregations and ministries throughout the church rely upon this seminary for well qualified and committed pastors, teachers, and leaders. The church and the public look to Luther Northwestern as a center of Lutheran theological reflection.

Now it reads: "Luther Seminary educates leaders for Christian communities: called and sent by the Holy Spirit, to witness to salvation through Jesus Christ, and to serve in God's world." There is an evolution here, and clear implications for our work together as faculty, students, and staff. The shift reflects an intentional broadening of our institutional vocation and our sense that public leadership in the church takes more forms now than it did in previous decades.

Hanan Alexander writes that "education is not about acquiring just any knowledge, but that which is worthwhile; and to judge the worth of something requires a vision of the good."[17] Part of what is sustainable and exciting about graduate theological education in our contemporary context is that we have a vision of the good—a shorthand, perhaps, would be "the reign of God." But we need to translate this vision, or at the very least embed it, within our understanding of the "good" in relation to our vision of theological education.

For many decades graduate theological education has been strongly shaped by the dynamics of scholarly guilds, by the shape and construction of higher education more broadly construed, and even to a certain extent by the rubrics of "scientific positivism" afloat in the larger cultural spaces. It is difficult to find a way to move within those forces with sufficient clarity and vigor. What would a curriculum look like that has at its heart "educating leaders . . . called and sent"?

Again, Alexander notes: "the purpose of learning is to enhance one's moral insight, not increase one's material worth; to become better at *living well* or *practicing a valued craft,* not at *earning a living.* Professionals who graduate from educational institutions require not merely *practical skill* but also *purposes for which to practice.*"[18] At the heart of the dilemmas we face in graduate theological education is the articulation of "purposes for which to practice" that are sufficiently compelling and resonant to students socialized in digital media culture.[19]

On the face of it, I cannot conceive of a more compelling educational "end" than Luther Seminary's mission statement. But I also know that many students find it difficult to figure out what we mean by "witnessing to salvation," particularly if we intend to do so "in God's world"—a statement that extends beyond the walls of the local church. A generation of people socialized within a mass mediated popular cultural context in which explicitly theological language was most often represented as belonging only to a few vehement fundamentalists must now work to find ways to reclaim explicitly theological language that has resonance with their own experiences and that speaks within their own contexts.

The opportunity here is vast, and can be recognized even in the commercial success that puts books such as Kathleen Norris's *Amazing Grace* or Roberta Bondi's *Memories of God* on the local mega-bookstore shelves and films such as *The Passion of the Christ* in the realm of financial blockbusters. People are hungry for language and experiences, for beliefs and commitments that are deeply rooted in historically grounded religious communities. For that hunger to be fed, however, they also rightly seek respect for their own positionalities.

Which point brings me back to the statistics with which I began this chapter: "currently there are more than 300 professional Catholic lay ministry programs in the United States with a combined enrollment of more than 35,000—about 10 times the number of seminarians in post-college studies, and 13 times the number of men in deacon formation programs."[20] I also noted my colleague's anecdotal reflection that "more people enter public leadership in the ELCA each year through nonjuridical routes than graduate from all eight ELCA seminaries combined." These statistics point both to the willingness of people to enter public leadership in their communities of faith *as well as* to their refusal to participate in graduate programs that do not respect who they are and the contexts in which they are embedded.

How can we take seriously each of the legs of the "trio of triads" I pointed to early in this essay? How can seminaries, in particular, but Christian higher education more generally, participate in bringing our enormous resources to the task of equipping and sending leaders for Christian communities? Lee Shulman lists a core set of competencies that "spiritual pedagogues" require:

> subject-neutral critical thinking skills that transcend disciplines and traditions, the subject-specific thinking of their own ethical tradition and of relevant cognitive traditions, familiarity with at least one empirical discipline that teaches the fallibility of its results, and appreciation for aesthetic forms of representation that celebrate creativity and hope. They also need what Shulman calls "pedagogic content knowledge"—intuitions learned from experience about enabling others to inquire as well as the inquiry skills themselves.[21]

Let me take in turn each one of Shulman's competencies. First, "subject-neutral critical thinking skills that transcend disciplines and traditions." As Shweder notes, before one can "think beyond another," one must first get inside that positionality, understand its core logics, experience its central emotions, live within its commitments. We must, to return to the Wiggins and McTighe rubric, help our students to develop the earlier elements of understanding before we require of them the more sophisticated elements.

At Luther we support the development of critical thinking skills by working with students to learn the basic "scales," if you will, of the tradition they will soon play with improvisationally. We still require our MDiv students, for instance, to take both biblical Greek and biblical Hebrew. These languages are then taken up into various Bible, theology, and leadership courses in ways that help students parse the central grammars of our tradition sufficiently deeply so as to be able to play with its margins and extend its translations. In this way the skills they learn are brought to bear across various disciplines within Christian higher education.

We also work with more than the cognitive, particularly in our requirement that students participate in Discipleship, a core set of courses that provide small-group Bible studies as a way to reflect theologically on their daily experiences. We require that all students participate in cross-cultural immersion experiences. This latter requirement grows out of an understanding that critical thinking requires a grasp of more than one's own context. Finally, we have worked for the past decade on establishing an Islamic Studies master's program at Luther. This program supports students who want to concentrate in that area, but is also a rich resource in the wider curriculum for supporting students' thinking across traditions. I am not arguing that all seminaries should do the same, but I *am* suggesting that it is crucial for our students who are called from and will be sent to communities of faith in a pluralistic world to have familiarity with how to engage respectfully in ecumenical and inter-faith dialogues, let alone in faithful conversation with people who have no religious community at all.

Shulman's second point is that students need "subject-specific thinking of their own ethical tradition and of relevant cognitive traditions." One entire movement of Luther's present educational strategy is the "interpreting and confessing" strand. This component of our curriculum seeks to develop within students a deep appreciation for, and a concomitant ability to confess within, their tradition's core faith witness. Many of the courses in this strand are quite similar to courses in ethics and history at other institutions. But our worship course is situated in this strand as well, and our senior biblical theology course is an "IC" course. These courses require students to work at the level of "feelings and actions" as well as "ideas." They also regularly draw upon leaders from outside the walls of the curriculum as teachers, or at least featured guests on a particular topic.

Shulman's third competency is "familiarity with at least one empirical discipline that teaches the fallibility of its results." This particular goal is perhaps one of the ones we have struggled with the hardest. Currently our curriculum includes a class at the beginning of each student's course of study entitled "Reading the Audiences." This course brings sociological theories, particularly in the areas of demographics and cultural studies, to the task of congregational study. Students are challenged to describe the community in which a specific church is located in numerical terms and with presentational charts that utilize spreadsheets and other more quantitative software. Many of our students find this course particularly challenging and resist the idea that such empirical work could have anything at all to do with proclaiming God's word. Yet a central issue in understanding statistics, demography, and other such empirical disciplines is learning how to critique and modify unstated assumptions. Such work teaches, as Shulman notes, "the fallibility of results," and is thus crucial to nurturing the deep humility that must always be at the heart of any Christian confessional stance.

"Appreciation for aesthetic forms of representation that celebrate creativity and hope" is the fourth of Shulman's competencies and is thoroughly embedded in Luther's explicit curriculum—in worship courses that study architecture, in Bible courses that utilize images as interpretive tools, in preaching and rhetoric classes that work with poetry and other forms of literature—but it is also present in our "implicit" curriculum. Daily chapel, for instance, is an important if yet implicit part of Luther's curriculum, and we strive to have this central worship experience draw on a multitude of aesthetic forms and frameworks. Music varies from elegant Bach choruses accompanied by full organ to more spare and informal praise bands. The cross is represented in a multitude of ways, from the large bronze crucifix permanently installed in our smaller chapel, to the Taizé painted crucifix that was temporarily in our larger chapel, to representations of the cross in myriad other media. We are also beginning to experiment more directly with digital media and with electronic representations.

The final competency Shulman writes of is "'pedagogic content knowledge' — intuitions learned from experience about enabling others to inquire as well as the inquiry skills themselves." This is by far the most difficult of the goals we have set ourselves. How do we support our students in conscious and intentional reflection upon their patterns of inquiry? How do we move beyond their own self-knowledge into helping them learn from experience in supporting others? We do not yet have full answers to these questions, but our own central intuition is that this kind of work can and must spread beyond the usual classrooms of a seminary. Already we are beginning to build relationships with churches, parachurch organizations, and other kinds of community institutions in which religious leadership flourishes. We have always had a "contextual education" component to our curriculum, but recently we are working to ensure that our entire curriculum reflects "learning congregational leadership in context."

As I have noted repeatedly throughout this essay, when the context around us is one of continual and rapid change, our educational leadership must be flexible, oriented outward, and deeply connected to the communities from which our students are called and to which they will be sent. This is a challenge that digital technologies can help us to meet, but only if we keep our eyes on the goals we're trying to reach. Hanan Alexander writes:

> Our very lives and those of our communities must become the intensive spiritual hothouses that summer camps represent. I call this *organic community* because there is a natural flow of complementary and mutually reinforcing ideas and ideals, study and practice, from the home to the neighborhood, the school to the synagogue, the youth group and summer camp to the cultural center and the social welfare organization. Communal norms can only be transmitted when the study, practice, and celebration of goodness is valued as highly by parents, grandparents, aunts, uncles, and neighbors as it is expected to be valued by their children.[22]

Although he is writing in a Jewish context, I believe Alexander's words are equally compelling in a Christian context. We know how powerful an impact Christian summer camps have on people. We can work toward a similar organic community that supports graduate theological education. Why is this important? Because we face in the broader cultural climate a context in which "reasoning by sympathetic identification" and learning embedded in practice is far more common than philosophical argument. Evangelism now does not look like a well-reasoned argument as to why Jesus Christ is our Savior. Evangelism now looks like many different things: a film by Mel Gibson, the music of U2, the melodrama *West Wing* on network television, WWJD bracelets, and Bill Moyers on television. Few of these examples are controlled by historically grounded, institutionally shaped communities of faith. There has been an explosion of energy in the last five years around using the World Wide Web to communicate faith, and hundreds of thousands of sites have emerged with all sorts of information—accurate as well as highly misleading or even false—on religion. When we attempt to build the "transitional community" that higher education can be (to use Bruffee's phrase),[23] we have to build that community mindful of the socialization our students have already encountered, and we need to speak in the languages with which they are most familiar if we are to have any hope of teaching them any others. We must also ensure that that community does not end at the seminary walls, and that the leaders we are educating will continue to educate us.

Here is where digital technologies hold such promise, for they make available to our classrooms—whether those classrooms are in typical buildings or structured online—the elements of the cultural context our students (and by extension, our communities of faith) inhabit. By thoroughly engaging media culture—respecting it as a powerful source of our students' meaning-making, and thus inviting it into our critical interrogation—we also attend more carefully to the world in which God continues to reveal Godself.

Paul once wrote: "But we have this treasure in clay jars, so that it may be made clear that this extraordinary power belongs to God and does not come from us" (2 Cor. 4:7). In a postmodern context those of us who tend to graduate theological education must at a minimum practice a deep respect for the meaning-making going on beyond our walls, continuing to be open to all of the ways in which the Holy Spirit continues to work within and among us. Only by doing so will we be able to support all those who are "called and sent by the Holy Spirit, to witness to salvation through Jesus Christ and to serve in God's world."

FOR FURTHER REFLECTION

Books

Brookfield, Stephen. *Becoming a Critically Reflective Teacher.* San Francisco: Jossey-Bass, 1995.

———. *Discussion as a Way of Teaching: Tools and Techniques for Democratic Classrooms.* San Francisco: Jossey-Bass, 1999.

Vella, Jane. *Learning to Listen, Learning to Teach: The Power of Dialogue in Educating Adults.* San Francisco: Jossey-Bass, 2002.

Films

Dead Poets Society. DVD. Directed by Peter Weir. Touchstone Video, 1989.
The Emperor's Club. DVD. Directed by Michael Hoffman. Universal Studies, 2002.
Mr. Holland's Opus. DVD. Directed by Stephen Herek. Hollywood Pictures, 1996.
The Hurricane. DVD. Directed by Norman Jewison. Universal, MCA, 2000.
Mona Lisa Smile. DVD. Directed by Mike Newell. Columbia Tristar Home, 2003.

Web Sites

Merlot (http://www.merlot.org/Home.po).
Tomorrow's Professor Listserv (http://cis.stanford.edu/structure/tomprof/listserver. html).
Wabash Center on Teaching and Learning in Theology and Religion (http://www. wabashcenter.wabash.edu/).

NOTES

1. "News," CNS news brief, *America,* September 10, 2001, 4.

2. Conversation in a Luther Seminary faculty forum, September 29, 2001.

3. This diagram is taken from their book. Grant Wiggins and Jay McTighe, *Understanding by Design* (Upper Saddle River, NJ: Merrill/Prentic Hall, 2001).

4. This is my paraphrase of Robert Kegan's quotation of Burbules and Rice's formulation of postmodernism. Robert Kegan, *In over Our Heads: The Mental Demands of Modern Life* (Cambridge: Harvard University Press, 1994), 325.

5. The Association of Theological Schools, *Fact Book on Theological Education for the Year 2000–2001* (Pittsburgh, PA: Association of Theological Schools, 2002).

6. Merriam Webster Online Dictionary, s.v. "context," http://www.m-w.com/cgi-bin/dictionary?book=Dictionary&va=context&x=15&y=15 (accessed May 12, 2004).

7. Thomas Boomershine, "Witnessing to the Faith: An Activity of the Media" (lecture, Saint Paul University, Ottawa, ON, May 1999).

8. Adán Medrano, "Media Trends and Contemporary Ministries: Changing Our Assumptions About Media," http://www.iscmrc.org/english/medrano.html (accessed May 12, 2004).

9. Elliott Eisner, *The Educational Imagination* (New York: Macmillan, 1985).

10. Parker Palmer, *The Courage to Teach* (San Francisco: Jossey-Bass, 1998).

11. Thomas Beaudoin, *Virtual Faith: The Irreverent Spiritual Quest of Generation X* (San Francisco: Jossey-Bass, 1998).

12. Palmer, *Courage to Teach,* 107–8.

13. Richard Shweder, *Thinking through Others: Expeditions in Cultural Psychology* (Cambridge: Harvard University Press, 1991), 108.

14. Shweder, *Thinking*, 108.

15. Shweder, *Thinking*, 109.

16. Shweder, *Thinking*, 110.

17. Hanan Alexander, *Reclaiming Goodness: Education and the Spiritual Quest* (Notre Dame, IN: University of Notre Dame Press, 2001), 173.

18. Alexander, *Goodness,* 173.

19. Please note: by "practice" I am not in any way making a theological claim about the outcome of our call. Rather, I am pointing to a logistical issue—what flows from our redemption on a daily basis? What are the fruits of the Spirit in this context?

20. *America,* September 10, 2001, 4.

21. Alexander, *Goodness,* quoting Lee Shulman, 186.

22. Alexander, *Goodness,* 205.

23. Kenneth Bruffee, *Collaborative Learning: Higher Education, Interdependence, and the Authority of Knowledge* (Baltimore: Johns Hopkins University Press, 1993).

Chapter Four

"You've Got Mail": Teaching and Learning in Online Formats

"All this nothing has meant more to me than so many somethings."

—Kathleen Kelly (Meg Ryan) to Joe Fox (Tom Hanks), *You've Got Mail*

In the Tom Hanks / Meg Ryan film *You've Got Mail,* the two main characters, Kathleen Kelly and Joe Fox, develop a close personal relationship via e-mail, without knowing that they are business competitors (even enemies) outside of cyberspace.[1] The e-mail process gives them room to explore who they are and to share their feelings with a degree of honesty that the rules of interpersonal etiquette do not allow in typical circumstances. The film is essentially a love story that uses e-mail as the main plot device. It's an interesting device, because even back when the film was released (in 1998), people were already aware of the ways in which e-mail communication was experienced differently, and that awareness has had both positive and negative connotations.

For the last several years I have worked in a variety of contexts trying to support theological educators who are attempting to integrate digital technologies into their pedagogical strategies. I have also taught a number of full-credit, graduate-level, semester-length courses in an asynchronous, online, distributed-learning format. I give you this context primarily for two reasons: first, to situate what I have to say, and second, because I am very conscious of how limited it is in many ways and of how rapidly the contexts in which we teach, and the technologies permeating those contexts, are changing.

Given this location, I am continually struck—sometimes with amusement and more often with frustration—by the singular intensity with which I am confronted by the same question over and over again. Whether I am working with local religious educators, seminary faculty, or faculty at research institutions, the primary question is always the same: is it even possible, let alone

63

appropriate, to be using digital technologies in the context of theological education? There are many versions of this question, and they arise from within these varied contexts with different degrees of intensity, but the question most often also comes attached to two underlying assumptions. First, the assumption is made that that phrase—"digital technologies"—is synonymous with desktop computers that are linked to the Internet, and second, that the only pedagogical strategy implied is online distributed education. The first assumption is one that I have problematized in earlier chapters; the second will flow through this chapter and the next. Having made these two assumptions, people find it very difficult to consider the integration of electronic technologies into theological classrooms with anything other than anxiety, because they fear that theologically focused learning has something uniquely and integrally relational about it to which we cannot attend in the "disembodied" context of the Internet.

This argument has two pieces to it that I would like to reflect upon. The first is the assertion that theological learning is uniquely and integrally relational, and the second is the assertion that online distance learning is by definition disembodied learning. If both of these are accurate, then the conclusion is inescapable: theological education cannot be done in an online, distributed way. On the other hand, if either or both of these are not wholly descriptive, then perhaps there is room for emerging technologies—even understood in this narrow sense—within our theological classrooms. It is probably obvious from my brief introduction that I will argue in this chapter that neither of these assertions is precisely accurate. Further, I believe there are ways in which online distributed learning actually forces us to attend to these questions more directly, and perhaps, at the moment at least, more creatively than more typical methods of teaching. Let me start with the question of whether or not online learning, particularly that which occurs in asynchronous,[2] distributed programs, is by definition disembodied learning.

IS ONLINE LEARNING DISEMBODIED LEARNING?

I think this concern has a number of obvious roots to it. We live in a cultural space—at least in the United States and in the middle-class, academic settings in which I work—that is increasingly a space of disconnection. Families are spread over larger and larger geographic distances and there is less and less public space available in most of our towns and cities (when was the last time you went to a public rally or even spent an hour in a *noncommercial* public space?). The mass media have become our most common form of "shared" communication. Yet there is an increasing sense of isolation and loneliness growing out of a "television commons" that is electronically produced by an ever narrower number of multinational corporations.[3]

Media literacy activists and communications scholars have pointed to the narrowness of representation and the channeling of attention that the square boxes with glowing screens in our living rooms and dens seem to call us to. And communities of faith have, for decades now, engaged television in particular with a skeptical, if not downright pessimistic, attitude toward any meaning-making engendered there.

Desktop computers have something very physical in common with television—that glowing, not quite square, screen across which race millions of electrons painting sharp pictures and sharing intense sounds. It is perhaps not surprising, then, that the underlying sense of disconnection and increasing loneliness that so many people feel in our contemporary context—and further, have identified as growing out of a televisual world—should be extended toward desktop computers and any worlds they might be responsible for engendering.

On a strictly physical or material level, "online" distributed learning, which is structured through such a screen, seems only the most blatant and obvious example of the decreasing amount of social relational space in our contexts. Now you don't even have to pick yourself up and move away from your home to come to a class. Now you don't even have to venture outdoors on your way to learning. Such learning seems only to contribute to the increasing marginalization of social relational community, particularly that experienced in historically grounded communities of faith.

These are important concerns, and I would be the last to suggest that we should not worry about the isolation and lack of complex and messy community in our midst. But if you listen to these common complaints, which on the surface, at least, seem to be so obvious and intuitive, there is much that we as theological educators ought to question. Those of us who work on faith formation, for instance, recognize that the deepest and most lasting religious formation occurs at home, in the midst of the family (however that is defined). There is no requirement that such formation be positive, but research suggests that it is lasting and deep, regardless of its contours.[4]

Why should we automatically assume that leaving home or work and entering a physical space labeled "classroom" should in some way automatically enhance learning? There is more and more attention being paid to the ways in which we have lost, in religious community, the sense of the "daily" and the "ordinary"—all those ways in which we identify and honor the Holy in our midst. I believe that the question we ought to be asking is how we can nurture and attend to learning that kind of learning, rather than accepting without question that learning that takes place at home has to, by definition, be problematic. Similarly, given the extent to which we in the middle-class U.S. context cushion our sense of relatedness to nature by running from our air-conditioned or heated homes to our air-conditioned or heated individual automobiles on our way to our air-conditioned or heated schools, why should we assume that venturing outdoors has any obvious learning component to it?

Beyond these material or physical observations of what we might be giving up comes the felt sense that sitting in front of computer screens and communicating only, or at least primarily in our current technology, via written textual forms has a distinctly disembodied aspect to it. We cannot yet see the people with whom we are communicating, and they cannot see us. The Internet joke that "on the Internet, they don't know I'm a dog!"[5] suggests that it is a process that is not only incidentally disembodying, but is essentially disembodying.[6]

But perhaps that objection is too broad and vague. Perhaps the underlying anxiety comes from our ability, when we are in front of these square, glowing screens, to be so drawn into what is occurring there that we forget about our embodiedness. We emerge, after an hour or two of intense computer work, with aching arms and an aching back and grumble in a confused way about the dangers of ergonomically inadequate computer workstations. Yet we don't stop to consider what was so compelling about the engagement that we were literally drawn out of our bodies long enough to acquire physical aches and pains that we only notice when we get up and try to move. Similarly, while there has been significant outcry about the amount of time that teens spend surfing the Internet and chatting with friends, less has been made about the concomitant observation that these same teens are watching less television in the process and may be more connected to friends.

Far from suggesting that online learning is necessarily disembodied, or unrelational, we might actually suggest, instead, that this emerging space for learning can be quite embodied and quite relational. As the character Kathleen Kelly notes in the film, "all this 'nothing' has meant more to me than so many somethings. . . . " We may have been discounting some of the more important benefits of online technologies, benefits that create opportunities for perceiving things differently. Indeed, as I have noted in earlier chapters, it can call into question our previous understandings of learning and of teaching and learning processes and spaces.

IS THEOLOGICAL LEARNING INHERENTLY RELATIONAL AND EMBODIED?

The other common complaint that I hear is that theologically focused learning is in some way uniquely and inherently relational and embodied and thus resists being put into a disembodied, "un-relational" environment such as the Internet. Here, religious educators have something useful to add to the discussion. Mary Boys, in her authoritative history of religious education in the United States, *Educating in Faith: Maps and Visions*, points to a number of different modes in which communities of faith over time have sought to educate their members. She notes four distinct practices in particular that span a spectrum from personal conversion in the context of affective revivals to transmissive, classroom-based didactic lectures aimed at uniformity of belief. This range of practices suggests both *more and less* "embodied" forms of pedagogy, depending on the context and the theological convictions of a specific group. How educators engage "the body" in learning clearly has taken different shape and form in different times and places.

The recent surge of interest in the structure of theological education in the academy, particularly in seminary or university contexts, has tended to take a fairly narrow view of "the body" in its investigations, which makes the current concern about "relational and embodied" pedagogies even more interesting. With the exception of some feminist voices and voices coming from communities traditionally marginalized in higher education, the shape and structure of theological education has been assumed to take place within traditional classrooms in traditional academic settings. While there has been some criticism of the fragmentation that that setting has created, the criticism has remained largely on the abstract level of theory and has rarely found ways into new visions for the actual practice of theological education. As Chopp notes:

> The ideas of *theologia* in Farley's work and of "schooling" in Kelsey's provide us with a kind of vision of what we lack and to which we aspire. But for both of these authors the constructive positions are formal, mediated neither through symbolic construction of faith nor through the particular structures of theological education. The strategies of most of the work on theological education thus far are ideational, formulating an abstract ideal to offer some vantage point of unity amid the fragmentation and pluralism.[7]

In most of the contexts in which I have taught, theological education was something primarily and ordinarily done in classrooms, with various kinds of texts, and engaging in various kinds of argument and textual evidential work. It has not been at all clear to me how "embodiedness" figured into that setting in any other than trivial or marginal ways. (Here I should note a major exception being work done within feminist theologies in feminist classrooms.) The primary educational technologies in use included not only chalkboards and overhead projectors, but the even more insidious technology of "hours," whereby classes met for a specified number of hours at certain times each week, and teachers and students had to fit their learning into that frame-work, rather than the framework evolving out of the necessary needs of the learning process.

Where subject matter under consideration had obvious physical compo-nents to it—worship, for instance, or pastoral care—such courses were rele-gated to the so-called practical arts (a phrase I have heard is that "practical theology is practically theology"). Students who required support for physi-cal differences had "adaptations" built into the learning process, but these adaptations were never considered to be potentially liberating for all students but rather necessary changes just for these somehow "disadvantaged" stu-dents.[8] Discussion of ideas that had obvious embodied consequences to them—sexuality, for instance, or hunger and homelessness—were either dis-cussed in quite "safe" abstract ways that had to do with overarching frame-works of moral reasoning or were, again, relegated to courses that were con-sidered somehow marginal to the curriculum. Indeed, it is precisely concerns about embodied knowing and contextual theology that, far from being central to the theological classroom, have been pushed to the edges. We need to be reminded of these issues, and we need to problematize *all* of the learning that is structured in theological classrooms. We need to ask deep questions of the whole system.

In the film *You've Got Mail*, Kathleen Kelly responds to Joe Fox's offhand "it wasn't personal" with a sharp "What is that supposed to mean? I'm so sick of that! All that means is that it wasn't personal to you. But it was personal to me. It's personal to a lot of people. And what is so wrong with being personal anyway?"[9] His assumption that business practices weren't predicated on per-sonal understandings is sharply contradicted by Kathleen's response, and I would like to "call" theological educators on their claim that online learning contexts are somehow inimical to theological learning by pointing out that our *typical* contexts are rarely embodied and contextual. I think we actually have more to fear and critique in our current classroom practices of *disem-bodied* learning than we do from our experimentation with online learning.

Either way, I believe that emerging learning technologies, even most nar-rowly and specifically construed as desktop-based asynchronous online dis-tance learning, have much to offer us by the way in which they call into ques-tion our current modes of teaching and learning. It is precisely because they raise these questions in sharp and new ways that we must engage them—and then bring the questions back into more typical classrooms as well. Given these conclusions, how might we consider theological education construc-tively in an online context?

My first answer is that backward design, as discussed in the previous chap-ter, gives us a valuable framework to begin from. That being said, it is also important to consider the ways in which we can recognize how embodied a form of education this kind of learning is—and help our students to attend to that embodiment. Yes, we bring our whole selves—body and all—to our learning, but that does not mean that we necessarily are conscious and reflective about that engagement. Even simple questions shed useful light on how we structure learning. For example, what kinds of software code produce what kinds of conversation online? That is to say, what are the mechanisms we are using to facilitate learning in online, asynchronous environments? Two of the most frequently used kinds of software—listservers and Web-based bulletin boards—actually construct quite different conditions for conversation.[10] To what extent are we as teachers choosing a particular mechanism because of the kind of learning it engenders, and to what extent are we choosing it because it happens to be what is available?

Think about the ways in which a conversation works via listserver, for instance. On a basic, material level, students do not need access to anything other than an e-mail account through which they can receive and send e-mail to participate in such a conversation. They can choose for themselves what e-mail client they will use, and they can organize messages in whatever manner seems most appropriate to their own learning. Course messages come into their mailboxes along with all the other mail that they receive and can be accessed at the same time. In other words, the course conversation enters their own context—they do not have to go out and enter it. The course conversation is also, to a much greater extent than is true with a Web-based board, under their control. They can compose messages in the manner in which they are most comfortable and familiar (in their own e-mail program, for instance, or cut and pasted from a different program; online while reading or off-line with queuing and sending at a later time). They can access and manage course mail just as they access and manage their other mail, filing it into whatever folders they might create.

As a teacher, I have the same kinds of options. I can use whatever kind of machine I might have access to and whatever e-mail program I prefer. I can have individual conversations with students just as easily as I have group conversations with the class. I am someone who is privileged to work in an institution where my computer is connected to an ethernet, and thus I access my mail several times a day without blocking my phone. In doing so, I have a good sense of when students are participating in the conversation without having to pay a lot of sustained attention to that question. I just gather that information as a side effect of flicking my eyes down my list of incoming messages.

A Web-based bulletin board, on the other hand, provides a different set of benefits and challenges. A tool like Blackboard, for instance, or WebCT (both of which are popular options in use across the country), creates a course conversation that is posted on the Web. To access that conversation, students and teachers must actively direct a browser to that site, enter it, and access the messages. Most such tools require quite up-to-date browser software, which in turn requires up-to-date hardware upon which to run, and, more often than not, speedy network connections. These requirements exert their own pressures. It is much more difficult, for instance, to download course conversation and work "off-line" in a Web-based bulletin board environment than in an e-mail environment. For students (and teachers) who depend on dial-up modem access and only one phone line, the decision to "go to class" is in some ways just as limiting as that found in the more traditional classroom space.

The constrictions of the "code"—that is, the way in which the bulletin board space is enabled via software coding to exist—narrow not only the choice of tools you can use to access the conversation, but also what you can do with it once you find it. Most such bulletin boards have predefined spaces within which you can write and respond to messages. If you find the space too small, you must cut and paste into several such spaces, fragmenting your message or even truncating it. It is also often quite difficult to download messages into one's own local computer for filing and management.

Yet, by the same coding, a Web-based bulletin board generally provides "threaded" graphic access to the conversation, allowing students and teachers to see at a glance how messages are connected to each other, thereby providing a ready history of the conversation and easy ways to check back on issues you want to revisit. In many of these programs it is possible for teachers to find out at what time, or for how long, students are accessing the conversation.

In different kinds of learning contexts, the benefits and challenges of these two very different tools will serve different pedagogical goals. Far too often, however, it has been my experience that teachers do not even consider these very embodied consequences of the code and simply use whatever an institution makes most readily available to them.[11]

Another example of the embodied nature of learning, and of how online, asynchronous learning makes that nature more clearly apparent, concerns what kinds of authority we are invoking and utilizing in our learning spaces. I frequently hear from other teachers—and struggle with myself—how much they miss having the body language clues they are used to in the typical classroom. Many of us believe that good teaching flows from the integrity of the teacher, and that authority is constructed in the "in-between" space between the resources the teacher brings to bear in a learning space and the questions that students use with those resources.[12] One of our most frequently used gauges of that "in-between-ness" comes through body language clues. Are my students engaged in the ideas we're struggling with? Are they present in the room? Is there some energy and excitement brewing? In a typical classroom I use body language clues such as body posture, eye contact, breath rate, and others to help me sense the answers to these questions. In an online environment I do not have those clues (at least, not yet).

I think that most of us in the traditional theological classroom rely on these same kinds of clues, using them even in lecture formats, to help bring materials alive for our students. We are so familiar with the process that we do not attend self-consciously or reflectively to those clues; we simply take them in along with everything else we are working with and teach accordingly. But when those clues are absent, rather than reflecting on other ways to get that information, other ways to answer these pedagogical questions, we are simply at a loss. We recognize that we have "lost a sense" of what is going on, but because we were not self-conscious and reflective about that sense in the first place, we don't have any idea of how to replace it.

I believe this dilemma poses an interesting set of challenges to the authority not just of teachers in a learning setting, but also to students. Early on in my online distance teaching I was struck by how apologetic students felt they had to be for not fully assimilating the materials we were reading before participating in a conversation. As we "talked" about the concerns they had, we realized that part of the problem was that in a typical classroom it was "OK" to show up not having done the reading, because you could always "show" by your body posture that you were engaged in the conversation. You could even "pretend" that you had done the reading by the way in which you piggybacked on other people's comments or sighed or giggled at appropriate times. While in an online learning space you can "piggyback" on comments, it is much more difficult to figure out how to sigh or giggle or simply have good "eye contact" so that other people know you're there.

That makes the assigning of reading, for instance, an interesting challenge in this kind of setting. What kind of reading will be engaging enough to be done so that it sparks questions and learning in itself? Given the vast amount of reading that is created by holding a conversation wholly in a textual format, what amount of "outside" assigned reading is really appropriate and manageable? What kinds of reading strategies do we want to model and support in our students? How can we be self-conscious about such modeling and support?

These questions ought not to be limited, however, to online settings. I am often struck by how many of my colleagues are frustrated by the degree to which their students "aren't doing the reading," or "don't know how to read," or "refuse to engage the issues." Yet rarely have I heard these same colleagues question whether or not their reading assignments were really all that appropriate. I think that we, as theological school faculty, have been so caught up in the modernist educational paradigm of "covering the field" that we are afraid to remember that all we can do is *support* our students' learning, we cannot *control* it. And we certainly will never be able in this current context— if we ever could in the past—to ensure that anyone "masters" a field of content. I think that a more realistic and appropriate goal is one of helping our students learn how to learn, how to sense the contours of a given field, and how to use its central tools.

My students' concern, however, was generally not so much about whether they were "mastering the content" but instead whether I understood that they were really trying to do the work. Rather than coming to the materials I was offering with the sense that they would engage them to see how they could be challenged and grow, how these materials might have an immediacy and appropriate sequence for them (crucial pedagogical questions), they were worried about how they were appearing to me and what impact that appearance might have on their grades. When learning is driven solely, or even just primarily, by such concerns, it is not learning that honors who we are and who we are becoming.

It was an online class, however, that created a new enough, or perhaps alien enough, atmosphere that this kind of discussion could emerge as part of the course content. Since then I have always named as one of the learning goals of any online course I teach, raising the self conscious educational questions. What does it mean to learn in this kind of environment? How do you assess what you are learning? How do you demonstrate that learning? How do you participate in a conversation managed this way? and so on and on.

Yet these questions should *also* be asked in typical classrooms. Teaching online has helped me to recognize that I need to get better ongoing feedback from students about their experience of the class, and I have learned that I need to do that in typical classrooms, too. Rather than assuming that I understand the body language of students gathered in front of me, I invite their comments in a written form at the end of each session and then provide feedback based on those comments at our next session. This is a method Stephen Brookfield developed called a "critical incident inquiry report," and it helps me to stay in touch with students.[13] Over time I have learned that I often misinterpret body language, mistaking active attempts to integrate for what appeared to me to be the silence of boredom. Or finding that what I saw as testifying to edginess with the discussion was instead a student's physical nausea from the flu, and so on.

We need to allow what we're learning and experimenting with in the online environment to permeate our more "traditional" modes of graduate theological education. If, instead, those of us who are working with online distributed education cling to our new contexts as a new form of expertise, we will seriously impoverish more traditional classrooms and lose the opportunity presented by emerging technologies to reshape and improve our more typical classrooms and other learning spaces.

Here is another example of how this can happen, drawing on the points I made in an earlier chapter about the importance of supporting all three kinds of learning in an online environment—cognitive, psychomotor, and affective. The cognitive is perhaps that element least difficult to continue to work with, given the extent to which text-based processes work well with certain kinds of cognitive modes. But what about the psychomotor and the affective? In typical classrooms I have tended to rely on small-group work and presentations as means of engaging students in these modes. But in the online environment I have had to be more intentional and reflective. In the past I have used a Web-based description of the Lord's Prayer dance anthem, for instance, to urge my online students to get up out of their computer chairs and try an embodied form of prayer as a way to prepare to enter our class.[14] The exercise also helped them find a useful Web site that engages issues of welcoming children to worship and supported a discussion in which we talked about how to help people learn something physical using just flat, two-dimensional images. This year, however, I decided that that exercise was not useful solely in the online environment, but that it actually was equally appropriate in my more typical classroom settings. I doubt that I would have even begun to question what I needed to do for psychomotor engagement in the typical classroom if I had not already thought about it in the online classroom.

Another example pertains to how I started to engage affective issues in the online learning space. Trying to find a way to help my students create an affective sense of community, to have a shared experience that had affective components to it, I asked them to watch a film as the assignment for the week and then enter into a discussion about it. Although each of them watched that film separately from their classmates (although not necessarily alone; in fact, most watched the film with friends and family), the film still provided enough of a shared experience that we entered into a passionate and lively discussion about it that created enough sense of "group" to carry over well into our other conversations. I was very pleased by how that assignment worked and have begun this year to think about how to create similar kinds of deliberate experiences in my more typical classrooms. Again, the online learning experience led me to rethink my typical classroom experience.

Yet another way in which online teaching has helped me rethink and reshape my typical teaching has been the desire to utilize the best of what the Web offers in terms of easy publishing. From the beginning of my online teaching, I was concerned that we find ways to share each other's ideas, and the projects upon which students were working, with a broader community.

Part of what I did was require that assignments be sent to me in a form that I could publish on the Web site for the class. In this way students could engage each other's work. But in this way we soon discovered that a larger public could engage their work, too. Indeed, an online learning space can be a much more public arena than a typical classroom, opening up resources and making them available far beyond the usual reach of a class. Such a space can also bring opinions and ideas from widely varied contexts into what is otherwise a more narrow context. Publishing student papers on the Web with a space that allows for comment and response builds in a level of interactivity that we have to work hard to create in a typical classroom. There are a variety of tools available now that make this kind of publishing relatively easy—weblogs and wikis among them.[15]

Indeed, in my current institution the faculty is working hard to contextualize our work in the communities of faith from which our students come and to which they will return. We are experimenting with "teaching congregations" and other kinds of models that enable us to move teaching and learning out of static classroom models and into more organically connected spaces. The Web is very useful here, as it is just as easy to publish student papers coming from a typical classroom on the Web as it is from online classrooms. But the Web also creates enormous opportunities for us to solicit conversation and reflection from the communities of faith that we hope we are preparing our students to lead. I doubt that I, at least, would have even considered doing so had I not first seen how well it worked in the online environment. Having done so there, I was eager to make the same richness of conversation and direct link to worshipping communities present in the more typical classroom settings within which I work.

There are numerous other examples I could offer, but at this point I will leave those to my Web site and other dynamic environments. Here I will simply reiterate that I am convinced that online, asynchronous distributed learning, far from being incompatible with relationally focused, embodied theological learning, actually is a crucial resource for invigorating and refreshing the more typical modes in which such learning is occurring in higher education in the United States.

Such teaching is not a passive resource, however, and it is not a simple "tool" that we can use in instrumental ways. As I wrote in the first chapter in this book, graduate theological education faces a set of challenges that require us to adapt, to engage the contexts in which we teach with as rich and complex a set of questions and creativity as we can muster. To return to *You've Got Mail*, here is a film that traces the growth of a powerful personal relationship fueled by both passion and forgiveness. In that sense it can provide some lovely analogies for thinking about prayer as the development of a relationship with God. What if we imagine our prayer as a form of e-mail correspondence with a largely unknown "other" who invites us into deeper honesty, for instance? What if we imagine ourselves as broken beings, clearly tempted into showing forth our "worst selves," and yet also forgiven, analogous to the ways in which Kathleen and Joe forgive each other? These are powerful metaphors for feeling our way more deeply into relationship with God.

Yet the film is not wholly unproblematic, for in the end, the subplot suggests that the swallowing up of the independent children's bookstore is inevitable, the consequence of a large, blockbusting chain store moving in as competition. That underlying story is largely unproblematized. There appears little alternative but for the little store to be swallowed up and its proprietor to fall in love with the newly humble owner of the large store. Such a story does *not* invite us into the social justice questions embedded in our increasingly "glocalized" contexts, for instance. Indeed, the one attempt to organize collective neighborhood action in the film *against* the chain store is portrayed as clearly failing, defeated by individuals' needs to pursue their own pleasures.

What we are called to is not a simple acceptance or rejection —whether we are talking about possible theological reflection on a single popular film, or the appropriateness of using digital technologies within theological education— this is not an instrumental challenge, but instead an adaptive one. We must find ways to invite each other into sustained reflection that is respectful of each others' needs and those of our communities. We must invite reflection on this "nothing" and in so doing problematize the "something" as well.

FOR FURTHER REFLECTION

Books

Blood, Rebecca. *The Weblog Handbook: Practical Advice on Creating and Maintaining Your Weblog.* Cambridge, MA: Perseus Publishing, 2002.
Horton, Sarah. *The Web Teaching Guide: A Practical Guide to Creating Course Web Sites.* New Haven: Yale University Press, 2000.
Kim, Amy Jo. *Community Building on the Web: Secret Strategies for Successful Online Communities.* Berkeley, CA: Peachpit Press, 2000.
Lessig, Lawrence. *Code and Other Laws of Cyberspace.* New York: Basic Books, 1999.
———. *Free Culture: How Big Media Uses Technology and the Law to Lock Down Culture and Control Creativity.* New York: Penguin Books, 2004.
———. *The Future of Ideas: The Fate of the Commons in a Connected World.* New York: Random House, 2001.

Palloff, Rena. *Building Learning Communities in Cyberspace: Effective Strategies for the Online Classroom.* San Francisco: Jossey-Bass, 1999.

Weinberger, David. *Small Pieces, Loosely Joined: A Unified Theory of the Web.* Cambridge, MA: Perseus Publishing, 2002.

Web Sites

KAIROS, A Journal of Rhetoric, Technology, Pedagogy (http://english.ttu.edu/kairos/index.html) (accessed May 13, 2004).

Mary Hinkle's Web (http://www.luthersem.edu/mhinkle/) (accessed May 13, 2004).

The Open Knowledge Initiative (http://web.mit.edu/oki/) (accessed May 13, 2004).

Resources for Christian Leaders (http://www.christianleaders.org/) (accessed May 13, 2004).

Stephen's Web on Knowledge, Learning, Community (http://www.downes.ca/) (accessed May 13, 2004).

The Visible Knowledge Project (http://crossroads.georgetown.edu/vkp/) (accessed May 13, 2004).

The Yale Web Style Guide (http://www.webstyleguide.com/) (accessed May 13, 2004).

NOTES

1. *You've Got Mail*, DVD. Directed by Nora Ephron. Universal Studios, 1998.

2. "Asynchronous" means "not at the same time" and is typical of classes that take place using Internet technologies where people access the course materials at different times from each other.

3. Lawrence Lessig, *Free Culture* (New York: Penguin Books, 2004), 161–68.

4. This recognition that early family experiences have a profound effect on the shape of faith over a lifetime has emerged from a broad array of research over the past decade. See, in particular, the Faith Factors research (http://www.faithfactors.com/index.htm), and the Search Institute research on developmental assets (http://www.search-institute.org/). Pragmatic curricula that utilize these findings include the work of the "Child in Our Hands" conference (http://www.youthandfamilyinstitute.org/conferences/cioh.html), and FaithInkubators (http://www.faithink.com/).

5. This cartoon, depicting one dog sitting in front of a computer talking to another dog, has become a classic statement of the concern.

6. This objection may well melt away in the next few years as increasing access to broadband technologies and visual forms of communication—programs like iSight—become available.

7. Rebecca Chopp, *Saving Work: Feminist Practices of Theological Education* (Louisville, KY: Westminster John Knox Press, 1995), 10–11.

8. Please note: being the parent of a child with physical challenges, I am very conscious of the ways in which those challenges are posed by an environment that assumes we are all capable of certain kinds of range and ease of motion. This context

does indeed "disadvantage" my son, but it is the context that does so, not something innate to him.

9. All quotations from the film are my own transcriptions taken from the DVD.

10. A "listserver" is a piece of software that enables e-mail messages to be sent to all of the people subscribed to the listserver at once rather than having to add e-mail addresses individually. Many people are familiar with Ecunet listservers or Yahoo group e-mail listservers. Most listserver software also provides access to archiving and automated subscribing and unsubscribing processes. A "Web-based bulletin board" is software that enables threaded, searchable textual discussions on the Web. Programs such as Blackboard and WebCT are familiar versions of such bulletin boards.

11. Tangentially, an excellent analysis of the ways in which software coding facilitates or impedes learning and innovation on the Internet can be found in Lawrence Lessig's book *Code*.

12. Note, in particular, Parker Palmer's description of the paradoxes of learning space design in *The Courage to Teach*, 73–77.

13. Stephen Brookfield describes critical incident inquiry reports, and other ways of managing this kind of inquiry, in his book *Becoming a Critically Reflective Teacher*.

14. A dance anthem version of the Lord's Prayer is available at http://www .worship.ca/docs/godkids3.html.

15. A "weblog" is a frequently updated journal kept on the Web. A good introduction to the genre can be found in Rebecca Blood's *Weblog Handbook*, or at her weblog (http://www.rebeccablood.net/index.html). As the WikiWay Web site points out, a "wiki" is "a piece of server software that allows users to freely create and edit Web page content using any Web browser. Wiki supports hyperlinks and has a simple text syntax for creating new pages and crosslinks between internal pages on the fly. Wiki is unusual among group communication mechanisms in that it allows the organization of contributions to be edited in addition to the content itself." The WikiWay Web site can be found at http://wiki.org/. Both weblogs and wikis can be implemented using a variety of different software programs, many of which are available as open source.

Chapter Five

All That We Can't Leave Behind: Learning from the Past in Engaging New Media

I've written in earlier chapters about some of the underlying concerns that theological educators ought to be reflecting upon when we engage digital cultures in our classrooms. Many of the ideas I am working with invite popular culture directly into our meaning-making. In the last essay I wrote about digital technologies more narrowly, engaging them primarily in the context of working with online pedagogies. Here I'd like to focus instead on the range of ways in which we can use digital technologies within more typical classrooms.

In this essay I will focus on three ways to engage "theology and digital culture," all of which have to do with typical classrooms and all of which are linked to my title for this chapter. "All that we can't leave behind: learning from the past to engage new media." What does that mean? First, I use it to suggest that in order to teach faithfully and well in our current context, we need to remember those who have come before us and honor what they have learned. There are many ways to approach such a task, but in this chapter I will do a brief survey of some of the ways in which the Christian community has approached teaching literacy, both for the ideas such memories might provide and for the warnings we ought to heed.

Second, I believe that learning from those who have gone before us suggests that we need to think in terms of cultural interventions. One of the top music albums from the year 2000 in the United States was a U2 album entitled *All That You Can't Leave Behind*. At the same time as that album was gaining airtime, there was (and continues to be) an underground movement within certain parts of the Christian community around a novel series, and a film adaptation of that series, entitled *Left Behind*. In both cases these pop culture "events," if you will, drew on quite explicit themes and images from

79

within Christian cultures. These were just the beginning; in the years since, there have been an enormous number of popular culture "texts" that use explicit Christian symbolism, ranging from television shows like *Joan of Arcadia,* where God is a central character, to Mel Gibson's film *The Passion of the Christ.* Many other events ask deeply religious questions, although not framed in explicitly theological language (films such as *The Matrix, The Lord of the Rings, Harry Potter*, and so on).

Finally, I believe that one of the central things we "can't leave behind" in the process of integrating digital technologies into theological education is the opportunity to witness to God continuing to reveal Godself in the ongoing creation of the world. For me, that witness requires an attempt to remain faithful to the life of Jesus Christ, and doing so in the midst of digital cultures poses some crucial challenges as well as some rich opportunities.

LEARNING FROM THOSE WHO HAVE GONE BEFORE

I originally became interested in questions of theology and digital technologies because of my earlier involvement in questions of media literacy, particularly in relation to media education within religious education. There is much that those of us who teach and learn in graduate theological contexts can glean from the work of literacy educators, particularly if we attend to the history of that work. It is clear, for example, that the promotion of literacy has a history intimately bound up with religious communities. Even a superficial historical query will note that the earliest communities in the Jesus movements, for example, supported literacy as a means for increasing communication amongst scattered house churches. Our surviving correspondence from Paul is one prime example of this: a correspondence that altered the shape of those communities and in the process began to articulate a systematic theological framework for what we would eventually come to know as Christianity.

Much has also been made of another pivotal point in literacy history, the invention of the printing press, which made it possible for an Augustinian monk named Martin Luther to fundamentally transform Christianity by making its central texts accessible to communities of faith in their vernacular languages. Were his ideas the crucial fulcrum for this transformation, or was the technology to mediate them the pivot? Historians are still arguing this question.[1]

A more recent example would be from the United States, where, in the late 1800s and early 1900s, literacy was heavily promoted by religious communities who rushed to teach people how to read, in part, argue Graff and Arnove, for "similar purposes of religious propagation, maintenance of political order, and the formation of a national character."[2] It has also been argued that Christian evangelical efforts to promote literacy as a means to spread the gospel led to the formation of the Sunday School union and its libraries, and that they, in turn, were the precursors to our public school system.[3]

The first two instances are so far behind us on the historical timeline that it is difficult to get more than the bare outlines of the literacy story embedded in them, and in these cases scholars have focused on understanding the ways in which literacy helped these religious communities to "write their own story" in their own words and from their own experiences. In the most recent instance, however, the Christian evangelical rush to promote literacy in the United States, we have far richer documentation (in part, courtesy of print), and thus a richer glimpse of both the achievements and the underside of these literacy crusades. It is this underside that I think we need to be particularly aware of in our contemporary context as we start to implement digital literacies.

Historians are beginning to alert us to the ways in which Christian missionaries, for instance, moving across the western frontier of the United States uprooted the children of native tribes, forcing them not to speak their own languages in the process of being "civilized" into English-language Christianity. Surely this kind of literacy campaign, which resulted in the deliberate suppression and even eventual loss of indigenous languages, is not the kind of literacy campaign we would choose today. These movements also tended to promote "alphabetic literacy," or literacy based on written texts, at the expense of oral and other modes of language.

In this instance religious communities were supporting literacy as a means to spread their messages, but in doing so they also often deliberately suppressed other messages. Literacy in this instance was a tool, a tool to "read" with, but not a medium in which to create original meanings. This distinction is important as we consider how to integrate digital literacies into theological education. How often have theological educators trivialized the rich language systems that our younger students arrive with on our doorsteps? How often have we refused to take seriously their attempts to use popular culture resources, for instance, to think theologically?

I noted in chapter 2 that people engaging media—at least those in religious communities—are struggling to find ways to ensure that we engage mass media with full respect for our own "subjectivities," in Freire's sense of that word. We are teaching young people about television, for instance, by having them create their own video documentaries about themes they care about. In the process of doing so, they acquire a critically engaged perspective about the ways in which "pictures *can* lie" as well as the ability to create their own messages to share with others.

Another example of this more creatively engaged mode of using mass media would be the currently popular VeggieTales series.[4] Whatever you think about the biblical hermeneutic of this series, recognize that it plays a crucial function in many U.S. families' lives by providing a way for them to integrate explicitly religious language and themes into the daily practice of preschool video watching. Interestingly enough, by drawing on pop culture references that would be opaque to preschoolers but obvious to U.S. parents (various episodes quote *Monty Python*, *Batman and Robin*, *Star Trek*, *Saturday Night Live*, and so on), the creators of the series have built themselves a cult following on many college and seminary campuses throughout North America as well.

What media educators are learning from Freire, then, is that we have to take seriously the ways in which people engage, resist, contest, and in other ways play with mass media. Media culture, which is increasingly digitally created and mediated, is the water in which we swim. It may even be, as Tom Beaudoin argues, the "amniotic fluid" of younger generations.[5] If you found my earlier point about the literacy advocates of the late 1800s and early 1900s in the United States convincing, you will understand that this approach to media education is sharply different because of the way in which it favors teaching people to "write" as well as to "read" in these media.

I am convinced that these lessons are crucial ones for us to take forward into the newly emerging realms of digital culture. We "can't leave behind" this hard-won knowledge. We need to think carefully and intentionally about how to support religious communities "writing" in our diverse and multiple cultures, not just "reading" them, even if the reading is intentionally a critical one. But the writing itself cannot be a process of pushing predetermined content, which might be one way to look back at the televangelists. There is legitimate concern within theological education about importing consumer values into religious communities when we engage media that thrive in consumer contexts. Just as the televangelists were convinced that they could use mass media as a tool to push their message and were not concerned at all about the ways in which the practices people use to engage television would shape the meaning they would create with the materials that the televangelists produced, we need to think carefully about the social practices that shape how we engage digital technologies.

Yet these practices are neither uniform nor unilinear. Instead they are multiple, diverse, and highly contextual. Several years ago there was a spate of Hollywood films about the role of television in our culture, and even in this small, constrained space (because only certain kinds of film can be financed) there was a fair amount of difference in the ways the questions were engaged. *EdTV*, for instance, gave a much greater role to the participation of the audience and suggested a much more positive engagement with media than did

The Truman Show or *Pleasantville.* How communities of faith engage popular digital cultures will be likewise quite various and dependent on the particular communities' mission and their theological commitments. That means that our preparation of leaders to serve in such communities has to be equally varied, giving our students a wide variety of conceptual frameworks and pragmatic skills with which to improvise.

At a minimum, I think we have to understand as we enter the ritual spaces circumscribed by these newly emerging technologies that the meaning we try to encode within them is not a meaning we control. Instead, we have to enter into the shared social spaces in which these technologies thrive and prepare not only to transform but to be transformed (which is, of course, at the heart of teaching and learning).

PEDAGOGY AS CULTURAL INTERVENTION

Indeed, this is the second piece I do not want "to leave behind," and it grows out of this paradigm shift I have been discussing. The emerging understanding that people engage media neither as passive recipients nor all-controlling authors suggests instead that we are collaborators in elaborate ritual. We have to understand our pedagogies and our theologies in cultural contexts, as cultural interventions.

As I wrote earlier, *All That You Can't Leave Behind* is the name of an enormously popular musical album by superstars U2, and *Left Behind* is the title of a series of novels and a film. The wonderful coincidence—as in "coinciding"—of these themes suggests to me that religious symbols and biblical narratives afloat in our larger cultural spaces are a rich source for theological reflection. If we are serious about preparing leaders for communities of faith—and many of us who work in seminaries, at least, have that as our mission—then we have to understand how our students' and our faith communities' imaginations are already being fed and shaped prior to, or at least concurrent with, any of our own deliberate educational interventions. Again, I do not think that that feeding and formation is linear, or that media are simply value-neutral tools that convey meaning. Rather, I think that digital media, in particular, form a "medium" in which meaning is grown; they form a database of sorts upon which we draw to construct meaning, including religious meaning.

The readers of the *Left Behind* series, for instance, may know next to nothing about "premillennial dispensationalism" (the biblical hermeneutic upon which it is based), but many of them respond favorably to the compelling narrative of the books, finding in them a familiar science fiction narrative that also takes seriously biblical themes. Before condemning their enjoyment—as

I have heard some of my colleagues do—I believe we ought instead to ask what is compelling about them and use the answers as entry points into deeper, more communally linked reflection. The same is true about other books such as *The Da Vinci Code*.

In chapter 3 of this book, I briefly mentioned the work of cultural anthropologist Richard Shweder. Here I want to return to his ideas to explore the ways in which we can engage digital cultures within theological classrooms that are more "typical" than are online classrooms.

THINKING BY MEANS OF THE OTHER

Shweder's first mode is "thinking by means of the other," by which he means seeing a culture as expert in a particular domain.[6] One consequence of this mode is a tendency to think of "culture" as all-encompassing; in other words, we all live in one culture, but various of us have particular expertise in certain aspects of that culture. From within this perspective, for example, anthropologists would point to particular peoples or tribes as having developed talents or skills that others neglected.

To play with this description for a moment, I would have to say that, at least within the schools in which I have taught, digital technologies are much more adept at utilizing sound (especially music), image (especially through film and other forms of photography), and other grammars of the "affective" than are typical graduate school pedagogies. It is hard to convey sound using chalk and a blackboard (it's not impossible—think about musical notation—but it's difficult). It is not a coincidence that in our contemporary cultural settings, it is television and the Web that are the "campfires" around which people gather to interpret the news of the day rather than within most churches or other religious institutional settings. These digital technologies (and television is more a digital technology than anything else) have proven to be capable of telling stories in far more compelling and sensorially rich ways than many of our traditional religious services. Generally it is precisely this powerful storytelling capability that makes so many faculty wary of using such media. We have worked long and hard to gain our capacity for critical thought, careful reasoning, and distanced logics. We are understandably reluctant to cede those abilities to what might appear to be techniques (if not technologies) that rely wholly upon them.

On the other hand, if we are to continue to share, continue to provide access to, the deep sacramental and other modes of knowing within our communities of faith to people socialized within digital media, then we must begin to find ways to build bridges at least, if not thoroughly utilize these media that have such affective reach. Adán Medrano has argued that religious communities' primary resources for engaging our contemporary context are our ritual, our sacramental, resources.[7] Not every religious community defines sacramental in the way I am familiar with it in the Catholic community, but each of us has, I believe, ways of engaging knowledge, practices of knowing, that stretch beyond the purely cognitive into the realms of music, image, bodily gesture, and so on. It is these resources that we need to draw upon in our contemporary contexts to make religious meaning newly accessible, to make our "databases," if you will, Y2K compliant. It is these cultural resources that shape our "expertise" in this first mode that Shweder names.

Seminaries ought to provide our students with access to the best of the newly available digital technologies—digital video, MP3 sound capabilities, and so on. Not so that our students can become yet more "screen pastors," but because these technologies are the "languages," if you will, in which God is *also* revealing Godself and in which our communities of faith are fluent. As someone who frequently consults around confirmation programs in local parishes, I can attest to how hard it is to get young people into deep discussion with their community's elders. But hand them a video camera and invite them to interview such elders, and the whole tenor of the process shifts. Suddenly they are interested, and suddenly rich conversations begin.

Tom Boomershine has argued that in an electronic culture we reason more by means of sympathetic identification than by philosophical argumentation.[8] I suspect that most teachers have already encountered this mode of reasoning when they find themselves stymied by students who seem unable to grasp the fine points of a theological argument until they see it embedded in a film. But sympathetic identification can and should be deepened, stretched, challenged, and engaged to be more than simple identification. One of the treasures we have to share from religious community with other cultural spaces is self-transcendence. This is the experience of such deep identification with others that one goes beyond oneself, that "neighbor" comes to include even those we define as enemies. We also have much to share about practices of attention, of shaping the ways in which we focus and attend through shared ritual. In recent years, even with the power of digital technologies, religious communities are still a resource during our most traumatic times of woundedness for precisely this reason: we know how to shape and attend to ritual experience. And of course, we have much more experience with inhabiting silence as a mode of knowing than just about any other community or technology in our contemporary context.

Thus, digital cultures could be perceived as "expert" in sound and image construction via electronic media, and religious culture as "expert" in meaning construction via silence, attention, discernment, and so on.

GETTING THE OTHER STRAIGHT

Shweder's second mode is what he terms "getting the other straight," by which he means trying to see the internal logic of a particular system.[9] This is what media educators often call the first step of media education. We teach about video by helping students learn how to make videos. We teach about film by helping them learn the grammar of film: how a long shot works, for instance, and what a close-up accomplishes; how music can be used to set a mood; and how rapidly paced edits can pack significant narratives into compressed time spans.

Technical skills are only a first step, however, because media educators also always ask about the social infrastructure required to make a system function. What kind of industry must exist to build the capital to finance a film, for instance? It is not a coincidence that more action films than comedies are produced every year in the United States. Rather, it is a function of action being able to be more easily translated across various geographic and cultural boundaries than humor. Films that can be sold in multiple international locations bring in more income to produce new films than films that can only be sold in one market.

In the United States in particular we must understand the social infrastructure of media through recognizing the role that advertising plays in funding our various media. Many commentators have noted that television programming exists, for instance, as a means to get people to watch advertising. Currently media literacy advocates are beginning to ask deeper questions about advertising. In what ways do ads function in our knowing, for instance? If they are not about providing information about products—and these days, very little advertising is strictly informational—then how do they function? To what are they appealing?

Sut Jhally and others have begun to argue that advertising is in many ways an attempt to access our "dreamscapes."[10] Packed full of images and tightly edited, most television commercials, for instance, can give you vivid insight into the yearnings and fears at the heart of various groups of people. Commercials for beauty products, for instance, while on the surface appearing to be straightforwardly selling various cosmetics, may actually be reinforcing feelings of dis-ease, a sense of lack of self, or an endlessly shifting self. They may indeed be "selling" not the beauty products themselves but rather the underlying fear that would presumably send someone in search of such a product. So, the argument continues, advertising is not selling "product" so much as it is attempting to create markets for products.

The distinction may seem too subtle to be important, but if communities of faith can begin to "read" such commercials as a means to identify deep longings and then pose from within our own frameworks of faith deeper and more substantive resources from which to meet—or even, conceivably, transform—such longings, we might be able to nurture a literacy capable of truly building faith while engaging mass mediated popular culture. As students begin to learn the basics of theological argumentation, it is often a fun—and illustrative—exercise to ask them to dig out the "argument" that a particular television commercial is making and to imagine what theological resources one could use to reflect upon that argument.

Questions of the internal logic of specific cultures, however, particularly of social and structural logics, ought not to be confined to media venues. We can and should ask similar questions of our communities of faith. The "internal logic" of a particular religious community is not defined solely by its systematic theology, but also by its administrative structure, the geographic and political contexts in which it is embedded, its participants' practices, and so on. What it means to be a Christian in Thailand, for instance, where the majority of that country's inhabitants are Buddhist, is different from what it means to be a Christian in the United States, where Christianity is often arrogantly presumed to be the "default" mode. Theological education takes place in a context of globalization, and we are seriously shortchanging our students if we do not take that context seriously.

Such an approach is particularly pressing with relation to specific kinds of digital technologies. Important questions, questions that have profound ethical implications, are being decided today on the political and financial level by people who understand at least a minimum of the internal logic of the Web. Religious communities have an enormous opportunity to make a significant difference in the ways in which the Web is regulated, for instance, or in the ways in which speech and meaning are treated there, right now. But how many of our communities of faith, how many of our graduate theological schools, are working on the ethical implications right now? How many are even offering courses that look at the basic internal logics of these systems? Perhaps one of the most important books published recently on these questions is Lawrence Lessig's *Code*. But how many seminaries are offering students a chance to discuss it?

Similar questions exist within our contexts for our students who are not yet fully "at home" in our basic religious understandings. In much the same way that they may want to ask us, as their teachers, to come to a better grasp of the "internal logic of media culture," we must ask them to delve more deeply into the internal logics of communities of faith. We can no longer assume that every student who enters a seminary program is deeply steeped in religious formation from childhood. Indeed, some have lived most of their lives outside of religious communities and find their way to us after a recent religious conversion experience. They are excellent learners, but they must be given the opportunity to learn the basics. In any event, learning how to "read" a group of learners is a task every teacher must take on, and if we can help our students to do that with each other in intentional and thoughtful ways, we are already helping to prepare them to take up leadership in other contexts, as well.

THINKING BEYOND THE OTHER

Shweder's third mode for thinking through others is what he calls "thinking beyond the other."[11] This has always been a perilous move in anthropology, because, as Shweder argues, anthropologists have jumped too quickly to deconstruct cultures, to move beyond them, without first understanding their internal logics, the modes of knowing they value and in which they are fluent. It is clear that we have often done the same in Christianity, for instance, by moving as missionaries into other cultures without first seeking to understand them with sufficient respect for their internal integrity.

The point I take from Shweder is that in order to be able to think beyond the other in this way, in order to be able to argue that we, as theological educators, have some concerns about pedagogies that utilize popular culture, for instance, we have first to understand the internal logic of popular culture. As media educators learned to our dismay with television, it was not helpful to think of mass media as a simple truck off-loading cargo. Using that metaphor, we ended up in many ways accomplishing the opposite of what we intended.

Still, that was Shweder's second mode, learning the internal logic. So what would his third mode be for us? I believe in part thinking beyond the other in this context has to include thinking about the ways in which our central narratives, our central rituals, shape a mode of knowing and being that offers important critique and perhaps even correction to such logics. We also need to be open to the ways in which digital cultures may help us think beyond religious cultures. That may sound like a very risky or even dangerous idea, but if we are centered in our faith, if we trust our confession of faith, then we can be open to ongoing conversion, to continual engagement with the transformation of religious community.

Many people have written about GenX skepticism about institutions, particularly religious institutions. Current exploration into the religious attitudes of GenY (or whatever name the next generation after would like to claim) suggests that they are less skeptical of religious institutions in general and more interested in basic catechesis. At the same time, however, they tend to be much more open to diversity and pluralism than many of our institutional communities of faith. For both of these generations, "thinking beyond the other" provides a way to attend to either skepticism or increased openness, because it provides a way to critique digital culture *and* to critique religious culture and at the same time to value and respect the integrity of each. To put it somewhat differently, I find that a lot of my work with my peers in parishes right now—people with young children—centers around helping them both to explore their doubts about religious institutions and yet at the same time nurture their children (and incidentally themselves) through religious practices grounded in tradition. Indeed, this "thinking beyond the other" moves almost inevitably into Shweder's fourth mode, "witnessing in the context of engagement with the other."

WITNESSING IN THE CONTEXT OF
ENGAGEMENT WITH THE OTHER

"Witnessing in the context of engagement with the other" is in part Shweder's attempt to take seriously the postmodern understanding of social construction, particularly in cultural anthropology.[12] It is his term for the ways in which contemporary anthropologists are increasingly convinced that there is no such thing as a disinterested observer, or an observer who has no impact on a culture and whose observation in turn has no impact on the observer. Rather, as physicists have known for years, all observation involves reality construction.

When we as theological educators begin to take digital cultures seriously, we can begin to see how we are constructing meaning *with* our students and in the process also constructing the future of communities of faith. Our students become in one sense our popular-cultural informants, just as we become their religious-cultural informants. They give us access to the digital surrounds in which they move and breathe and have their being, and we do the same with the religious surrounds—including the print-based, philosophical ones—that we are embedded in. Ultimately, we ought to be able to witness, in the full religious meaning of that word, in both these contexts and more to come.

The best example I can think of for this kind of mutual witness is drawn from the Web. Wayne Dunkley is an artist who has been exploring the permeable boundaries, the intimately co-creating and mutually witnessing space, of experience and the Web. Entitled *Share My World: A Photographic Study on Race and Perception*, the site creates a three-dimensional engagement via the Web.[13] Dunkley created a photographic self-portrait and put it up in multiple locations and with various notations in and around Toronto. He then went back over time to those sites and photographed what was done with his pictures. Next, he published photographs of the "amended" posters on the Web along with a number of short autobiographical narratives. Finally, he created space on the Web site for people to respond to the process, and he incorporated their responses into the site. It's a site that continues to grow and is one of the best pieces of art I've found for helping students think about race and racism in the North American context. It is a site that both "reads" and "writes" in vivid cultural detail.

Obviously I have been stretching Shweder in some ways here, at least to the extent to which I have been posing digital culture and religious culture as in some ways separate and discrete entities. They are not, and I think Shweder's fourth mode makes that clear if nothing else does. We all live in digital environments, even theological school faculty, and we all live in religious environments, even those of our students who had no prior experience of religious community or even religious emotions until the conversion that led them through our doors.

Thus far two points: "all that we can't leave behind" means we need, first, to learn from what other literacy advocates within religious communities have done, and second, we need to keep in mind that digital technologies are cultures that we are embedded in, not just tools we use.

My final point is my briefest: "all that we can't leave behind" also means *for me* those essential elements of the Christian witness that are central to my faith life. These elements have to be a part of my creation and support of teaching and learning environments, whatever the context, whatever the culture. Now, perhaps more than ever in recent history, the lines between what is confessional or missional and what is "simply" educational, are blurring. With the advent of a social construction of knowledge perspective, or, to use the language I have used here, with the advent of "witnessing in the context of engagement with the other," there is more room to live in the interstices, to walk the balance beam I noted earlier in this chapter between the theological disciplines and the social sciences.

For me that has meant, in particular, always trying to keep the witness of Jesus Christ at the heart of my teaching and learning. Increasingly that witness has drawn me—compelled me, really—to think about the ways in which digital technologies engage the margins. There are vivid opportunities here—communicating something globally, for instance, requires a much smaller capital investment if I use the Web than it does if I want to use broadcast television.

But there are myriad cheerleaders for the opportunities; I am much more concerned about the challenges. How do digital technologies, for instance, direct me away from caring about those on the margins of our society? It is possible to construct a world of meaning using digital technologies that completely ignores those on the margins. I inhabit a very privileged space in U.S. culture. I have advanced educational degrees, my partner and I own a home together, our children are already fluent with using a computer. I can take my laptop anywhere in my house—anywhere within several hundred feet of my house, actually—and, via its wireless technology and the magic of a DSL line, connect to the Internet at very high transmission speeds.

Getting information, buying plane tickets, listening to the latest music, or in my kids' case, previewing the *Harry Potter* film trailer, are all possible at the click of a mouse button. This same technology makes it possible for me to read global newspapers, to keep track of how to support legislation that advocates for the poor are sponsoring, and so on. Yet it is a very beguiling technology, because it makes such access seem effortless. It makes it seem possible for me to control my environment to a large extent. It makes it seem possible for me to choose how and with whom my children and I will interact. I am convinced that such control is at its core illusory, but it is a highly seductive illusion, and it comes at a high price, not the least of which is the maintenance of a consumer society infrastructure that produces more waste and environmental damage than any other culture on Earth. It is an infrastructure that guides my eyes away from those on the margins and makes it uncomfortable to remember the structures upon which my privileges rest. I need, more than the first two of Shweder's modes, the second two. I need his mode of thinking beyond the other to help me continue to engage scripture to remember, literally re-member, the body of Christ. And I need his fourth mode, witnessing in the context of engagement with the other, to keep me honest and respectful in the process of playing and working across multiple cultural boundaries.

I need to find ways to help myself always attend to the challenge to clothe the naked, feed the hungry, offer drink to the thirsty. Perhaps even more specifically here, to make access to digital culture an access that everyone, especially those most marginalized, can attain. Some people may well argue that the best way to challenge this structure and the oppressive system of privileges it constructs is not to participate in it at all. There have certainly been religious communities that have argued that we need to refrain from television, for instance. But I am already too much a part of these cultural spaces to ignore them or to pretend that I am untouched by them.

Further, I believe that God continues to reveal Godself in all times and in all places. For me, refusing to participate suggests that God cannot be present. Rather, I am trying very hard to maintain what Brueggemann calls an "exilic language," participating in the wider cultural spaces but always trying to remember my mother tongue.[14] In the process, I construct different ways of inhabiting the wider spaces, and perhaps reconstruct them as well. Indeed,

I hope that I am being faithful to Shweder's fourth mode, witnessing in the context of engaging the other.

"All that we can't leave behind," then, has at least these three elements: a commitment to learn from those who have come before us, particularly to learn how to support creativity in new media; it means an understanding of "theology and pedagogy" that is at heart about attempting cultural intervention; and it means, finally, the attempt to live faithfully in the middle of digital cultures. If we, as teachers in higher education institutions—particularly those of us who teach in seminaries—can do this, then I think that teaching in digital cultures may indeed become a new and powerful articulation of core beliefs that resonates in learning communities that span generations.

FOR FURTHER REFLECTION

Books

Brown, Dan. *The Da Vinci Code.* New York: Doubleday, 2003.
Lahaye, Tim, and Jerry Jenkins. *Left Behind.* Wheaton, IL: Tyndale House Publishers, 1995.

Web Sites

Cormode, Scott. *Transforming Christian Leaders.* http://www.christianleaders.org/ (accessed on May 13, 2004).
Dunkley, Wayne. *Share My World: A Photographic Study on Race and Perception.* http://sharemyworld.net/ (accessed on May 13, 2004).
Valparaiso Project on the Education and Formation of People in Faith. *Practicing Our Faith* (http://www.practicingourfaith.org/) and *Way to Live: Christian Practices for Teens* (http://www.waytolive.org/) (accessed on May 13, 2004).

Media

The Ad and the Ego. DVD. Directed by Harold Boihem, Parallax Pictures, Inc., 2004. More information available at http://www.parallaxpictures.org/AdEgo_bin/AE000 .01b.html (accessed May 13, 2004).
Dretzin, Rachel, and Barak Goodman, producers. "The Merchants of Cool," an episode of *Frontline,* PBS, February 27, 2001. This episode is now available via the Web at http://www.pbs.org/wgbh/pages/frontline/shows/cool/ (accessed on May 13, 2004).
EdTV. DVD. Directed by Ron Howard. Universal Studios, 1999.
The Harry Potter Trilogy. DVD. Directed by Chris Columbus (1, 2) and Alfonso Cuarón (3). Warner Home Video, 2001–2004.

Joan of Arcadia. Broadcast television show. Written and produced by Barbara Hall, 2004.

The Matrix. DVD. Directed by Larry Wachowski and Andy Wachowski. Warner Studios, 1999.

The Lord of the Rings Trilogy. DVD. Directed by Peter Jackson. New Line Home Video, 2001–2004.

The Passion of the Christ. DVD. Directed by Mel Gibson. Icon Productions, 2004.

U2. *All That You Can't Leave Behind.* CD. Polygram Records, 2000.

VeggieTales. Assorted DVDs. Warner Home Video (more information available at http://www.bigidea.com/).

NOTES

1. Elizabeth Eisenstein, *The Printing Revolution in Early Modern Europe* (Cambridge: Cambridge University Press, 1983).

2. Graff and Arnove, cited by Kathleen Tyner, *Literacy in a Digital World* (Mahwah, NJ: Lawrence Earlbaum Associates, 1998), 19.

3. Mary Boys, *Educating in Faith: Maps and Visions* (San Francisco: Harper and Row, 1989), 31.

4. VeggieTales is a series of digitally animated 30-minute videos developed for preschoolers that seeks to illustrate biblical themes, either directly as biblical stories acted out by animated vegetables, or through narratives based on biblical themes. More information is available at http://www.bigidea.com/. The videos are so popular in the United States that you can buy them from mass-market stores such as Target and Walmart as well as through Christian bookstores.

5. Thomas Beaudoin, *Virtual Faith: The Irreverent Spiritual Quest of Generation X* (San Francisco: Jossey-Bass, 1998).

6. Richard Shweder, *Thinking through Others: Expeditions in Cultural Psychology* (Cambridge: Harvard University Press, 1991), 108.

7. Adán Medrano, "Media Trends and Contemporary Ministries: Changing Our Assumptions about Media," http://www.iscmrc.org/english/medrano.html (accessed May 12, 2004).

8. Thomas Boomershine, "Witnessing to the Faith: An Activity of the Media" (lecture, Saint Paul University, Ottawa, ON, May 1999).

9. Shweder, *Thinking,* 109.

10. Sut Jhally, Stephen Kline, and William Leiss, *Social Communication in Advertising* (London: Routledge, 1997), 301.

11. Shweder, *Thinking,* 109–10.

12. Shweder, *Thinking,* 110.

13. Wayne Dunkley, *Share My World: A Photographic Study on Race and Perception,* http://sharemyworld.net/ (accessed on May 13, 2004).

14. Walter Brueggemann, *Cadences of Home: Preaching among Exiles* (Louisville, KY: Westminster John Knox, 1997).

Chapter Six

Embodied Pedagogies: Engaging Racism in Theological Education and Digital Cultures

In the past several chapters I have tried to take up issues of pedagogy in theological education that are particularly pertinent to digital cultures and digital technologies, more specifically. I have suggested ways to think about what we do in theological education—our goals, our epistemologies, our frameworks for learning design, some of the particular issues inherent in digital technologies—and one of the central themes interwoven amongst all of these essays has been the embodied nature of our learning and reflection.

One of the reasons why I find the work of feminist theologians and theologians from marginalized communities so powerful is precisely because they have long been attentive to this element of theological reflection—our embodiment—and particularly sensitive to the ways in which specific embodiment (being female, being "of color") can be grounds for trivialization or dismissal of presence. Throughout my earlier essays in this book I have repeatedly tried to problematize the notion that digital technologies are somehow essentially "disembodying," although in some ways they clearly can help us to "get beyond" certain aspects of our bodiliness. We can transcend geography or time, for instance, in asynchronous learning, or we can subvert preconceived interpretations of body language.

There is one particular set of issues, however, associated with our "embodiedness" that deserves an exploration devoted to its specific dynamics, and that is the case of engaging racism in the theological academy, particularly by those of us who carry white skin privilege. There are some profound ways in which digital technologies can invite people into meaning-making in ways they would not otherwise be immediately open to. I can think of several course conversations, for instance, that sprang up when one or another of my students assumed that the whole class was white (a common assumption on the part of many white people), when in fact it was not. But I think there are many ways in which digital technologies might simply "re-inscribe" such biases as well.

So it is, now, to these issues that I turn. I need to begin in a more personally revealing tone, for I am situated very specifically and must speak from that location. I am a white and middle-class citizen of the United States living in a predominantly white and middle-class neighborhood in the United States and teaching at a predominantly white and middle-class seminary in the United States. Slowly, painfully, I am coming to recognize the stark contradictions and silently violent tolerance present in the communities I grew up within, and within which I still find my home. How is it possible to hear the gospel and at the same time "know" that people of color are "naturally" more poverty-stricken, or "naturally" more violent, or "naturally" less sophisticated in their theologies?

These are the kinds of knowledge, I'm slowly beginning to recognize, that have permeated my worldview. Intellectually I don't believe any of these statements; I abhor them. And when I see a strong, young black man walking down the street toward me, I do an internal calculus—is this someone to be afraid of? My next thought is to recognize that calculus and name it as racist, but it nonetheless happens. Another example: I have heard myself describe an African-American philosopher as "an incredibly brilliant black woman." When was the last time I described a white philosopher as "an incredibly brilliant white woman"? The institutionalized racism of the United States has seeped into me from birth, it has "formed and transformed" me at a very deep level. This is a very painful example of a "null" curriculum operating.[1]

In a U.S. context where the history of the civil rights movement is being rewritten, where we cannot even maintain the most basic and humble of affirmative action programs, where the poverty and degradation facing people of color in this country is growing exponentially every day, people of faith—white people of faith—must act; we must unpack our complicity in the structures of oppression and transform our formation. We must think about how and why and what we know in our very bones about white dominance, and we must reconfigure the destructive, destroying aspects of that epistemology. Given the existing "digital divide" between predominantly white communities and communities of color, is it even possible to promote the use of digital technologies within theological education?[2]

My primary answer is of course it's possible, but only if white theological educators consciously bring antiracist pedagogies into our teaching. Indeed, in some ways my answer to this question mirrors my answer to the question of whether or not digital technologies can be used within theological education more generally—yes, of course, but only if we are intentionally reflective about how we do so.

NONFOUNDATIONAL KNOWLEDGE

"Nonfoundational knowledge," writes Bruffee, is

> an alternative to this traditional, cognitive, foundational idea. It assumes that knowledge . . . is a community project. People construct knowledge by working together in groups, interdependently. All knowledge is therefore the "property" not of an individual person but of some community or other, the community that constructed it in the language spoken by the members of that community.[3]

This is a definition that has much in common with the Palmer ideas I broached in chapters 1 and 2 of this book. It suggests that at any given point any one person is a member of many diverse "knowledge communities." This description may seem awkward, or even contradictory, at first, but upon reflection it is quite useful for describing contemporary experience. The graduate theological frameworks that use words like "hermeneutics" and "epistemology" are one set of languages for describing contemporary experience that make it possible for me to converse with scholars across the United States about the dynamics of religious experience or the intricacies of popular culture. When I am speaking with my friends about our favorite television show or discussing what hymns to choose for a Sunday liturgy, I use very different words. My most difficult personal struggle is often to make sense of these very different languages. Am I talking about utterly dissimilar things, or is there some kind of narrative thread that ties them together? A framework that describes knowledge creation as social and embedded in knowledge communities is not only descriptive of my personal experience but also suggests some very important questions that need to be asked.

One question we must ask within theological education, a pressing question whether we are talking about media cultures more generally or racism in particular, concerns the centers of power that structure graduate theological education. What are the "discourses" I'm attempting to work within? To which knowledge communities am I drawn, and why? As a professor teaching in a Lutheran seminary, my answers to these questions are many. I want to be able to "speak the language" of religious education—both in the contexts where it is most often practiced and in the academic corridors where it is researched. I want to have a biblical imagination and some degree of theological complexity. I want to be fluent in the languages of higher education. I want to be able to have a voice in the larger professional organizations to which I already belong (APRRE, AAR/SBL, CTSA, and so on). But I also want to hold on to the languages I flourished in prior to my entrance into academe. I need the energy, critique, and vision of the very diverse feminist community that's nurtured me all these years. I need the ritual, the sacramentality, the global community that is the Catholic Church. I need to be able to continue to make sense to my extended family, to the base communities I've been involved in over the years, to my longtime friends and partners in activism. And more than anything, I want to be able to give something back to these communities that have nurtured me.

Bruffee eloquently summarizes my dilemma: how am I to value the knowledge communities from which I've come while still gaining fluency in those to which I'm drawn? In considering the differences between the two lists noted above, one characteristic is starkly present to me: the former list privileges one particular kind of knowing, one set of "languages"—and with the possible exception of practitioners of religious education, they all "speak" in academic English—while the latter list is more varied and supportive of ways of knowing that emerge in words of passion, commitment, liberation, love.

Yet even the driest academic English has found ways to speak to Christian commitment. Even the most arcane prose deconstructs patriarchal institutions and attempts to reconstruct a more just community. I have had the opportunity in my academic work to study feminist theology, to speak of "transformative pedagogies," to study the delicate inner dynamics of spirituality. Much of the work I've done, the books and articles I've read, tries to maintain a connection between theory and practice, tries to embody "praxis" in quite sophisticated ways.

Yet what does it mean that in years of work within theological education, while I've read extensive treatments of sexism in theology, I haven't read similarly sophisticated treatments of racism in theology? It is not because they are not available. West, Cone, Eugene, Walker, and many others have offered trenchant critiques from within a Christian and academic context. And I don't think it's because I or my colleagues are trying to deny that racism exists. On the contrary, writers such as Groome cite it as one of a number of unjust dynamics Christians need to encounter and fight against. I think the problem is a more thoroughgoing one: the academy in the United States is fundamentally structured, like most of U.S. culture, in support of white supremacy. The professional context I'm drawn to—research and writing in the area of religious education—is a knowledge community fundamentally structured in support of white supremacy.

Does that mean that it's a community that practices blatant racism? Far from it. Overt racism carries very strong sanctions, particularly within an academic institution. But subtle racism, the kind that supports a knowledge community that is unaware of its "whiteness" and the extent to which its practices and languages support that "whiteness," is pervasive. With thanks to McIntosh, I have started to try to identify the privileges that accrue to me because of the color of my skin. McIntosh writes:

I was taught to see myself as an individual whose moral state depended on her individual moral will. My schooling followed the pattern my colleague Elizabeth Minnich has pointed out: whites are taught to think of their lives as morally neutral, normative, and average, and also ideal, so that when we work to benefit others, this is seen as work which will allow "them" to be more like "us."

I decided to try to work on myself at least by identifying some of the daily effects of white privilege in my life. I have chosen these conditions which I think in my case attach somewhat more to skin-color privilege than to class, religion, ethnic status, or geographical location, though of course all these other factors are intricately intertwined. As far as I can see, my African-American co-workers, friends and acquaintances with whom I come into daily or frequent contact in this particular time, place, and line of work cannot count on most of these conditions.[4]

McIntosh's list is long. I will quote four of her recognitions that struck me as powerfully true in my experience and then add some that I am struggling to articulate in the context of a graduate theological education:

13. I can speak in public to a powerful male group without putting my race on trial.

14. I can do well in a challenging situation without being called a credit to my race.

15. I am never asked to speak for all the people of my racial group.

16. I can remain oblivious of the language and customs of persons of color who constitute the world's majority without feeling in my culture any penalty for such oblivion.[5]

I will add:

a. When I assign required texts from the central figures in my field, I can assume they share my skin color, unless otherwise noted. (For example, unless I am teaching about "liberation theology" or "black theology.")

b. When I sing a hymn or say a prayer, my skin color is equated with "purity" and "goodness" rather than with "evil" and "sin."

c. I can assume that liturgies that use the body language and images I grew up with do not need to be "enculturated" to be reflective of people who share my skin color.

d. I can assume that the research whose theories I use in my work (for example, "stages of faith development") was done primarily with people who look like me.

These are simply a few of the signs of white supremacy that occur to me as I try to think about this. They are material conditions, ever-present background to my academic context. But I do not cite them to "get myself off the hook," to somehow suggest that the problem is too difficult for any one individual to engage. Far from it! As I hope the beginning of this chapter makes clear, I have already begun the painful process of "consciousness raising." There are always opportunities to work on these issues. And it is possible to make analysis of racism a central focus in settings where it has not been before. All I am recognizing is that I have not done so, at least not in the focused and central way I would like to.

Why not? There are many answers to that question. On a professional level, dismantling racism has not carried the same incentives in my academic socialization as "learning the literature" has. Developing a philosophy of religious education, understanding developmental psychology, mapping the history of educational practices—without specific attention to the social construction of race—these are all content issues I must be responsible for within my seminary and my larger guild of religious education.

Frankenberg, whose qualitative research on the construction of whiteness among women is exemplary, suggests that there are currently three ways in which the white women she studied understand themselves in relation to racism. She identifies them as "essentialist racism," "color and power evasion," and "race cognizance." "Essentialist racism" is the discourse white people most often recognize as racism. It is a framework for understanding difference that assumes a hierarchical, "essential, biological inequality."[6] Early in U.S. history, this is the language in which the category of "race" was developed. Yet it is by no means a historical artifact, for it can be found reemerging in the current "bell curve" hypotheses of Murray and Herrnstein and in certain versions of social policy.

The second moment of discourse Frankenberg labels "color and power evasion." She describes this language for managing difference as one that asserts "we are all the same under the skin . . . culturally we are converging . . . materially we have the same chances in U.S. society . . . any failure to achieve is therefore the fault of people of color themselves."[7] This second language for managing differences in skin color suggests that any differences have not been, nor should they be, materially relevant, although they may perhaps provide an interesting texture to our common life. I believe that it is this second language that is most often implied in practices of "liberal tolerance." This is clearly an improvement over "essentialist racism" in its assertion that organizing life in raced categories is not appropriate, but it ignores the substantial ways in which white people continue to internalize and institutionalize dominance structured by race.

The third way in which the white women whom Frankenberg studies tried to "think through race" was in terms she labels "race cognizance." That is, these women insist once again on difference, but in a form very different from that of the first moment. Where the terms of essentialist racism were set by the white dominant culture, in the third moment they are articulated by people of color. Where difference within the terms of essentialist racism alleges the inferiority of people of color, in the third moment difference signals autonomy of culture, values, aesthetic standards, and so on. And, of course, inequality in this third moment refers not to ascribed characteristics, but to the social structure.[8]

The difference between these latter two forms—color and power evasion and race cognizance—helps to elicit the distinctions between "multicultural education" and "antiracist" education. Grinter distinguishes between the two forms of education when she writes that

> multicultural education believes in the perfectibility of the existing social structure, and assimilation of its component cultures into a social consensus with shared values. . . .
>
> In contrast, anti-racist education believes in the reality and significance of conflict in a social system that concentrates power in White, middle-class and male hands, and which discriminates against other groups on grounds of their inadequacy or incompetence. . . .
>
> . . . [M]ulticultural education believes in long-term educational policies that persuade individuals to change their attitudes towards other people and their culture. Racism is seen as an unfortunate personal aberration, based on ignorance and misunderstanding which can be countered by accurate information. . . .
>
> Anti-racist education, in contrast, sees racism as an organizing principle of the social and political structure, closely linked to a system of class and other forms of discrimination that deny human rights: an artificial construct designed to facilitate and perpetuate inequalities. . . ."[9]

I believe my professional socialization has been structured most intently by the second mode suggested by Frankenberg, that of color and power evasion. It has far more often tried to be multicultural instead of being antiracist. Although Frankenberg and Grinter were writing at the dawn of the Web, before it was widespread in use, similar dynamics persist among digital cultures. L. Nakamura, who has written extensively on the social construction of race in digitally mediated environments, labels color and power evasion in cyberspace as "cosmetic multiculturalism" that promotes "a false sense of racial equality—or post racial cybermeritocracy—that actively works to conceal 'the entrenched racial problems of black and white America.'"[10] Yet she, like Frankenberg, also identifies a form of engagement with race that has the potential to be antiracist. Such engagement she labels a "vexed multiculturalism" that appears in a variety of places, including the film *The Matrix*, where Nakamura identifies a future world that is "emphatically multiracial; rather than a place where race has been 'transcended' . . . a world in which race is not only visible but necessary for human liberation."[11] I think she is working with a concept very similar to Frankenberg's "race cognizance," and indeed she argues for similar kinds of self-reflection and critical engagement across a variety of boundaries.

Although there was early euphoria about the possibility of the Web transcending race, careful cultural studies scholars are concluding that such optimism remains more akin to the multiculturalism Grinter identifies rather than the antiracism she urges we must pursue. Is this distinction important? Is it even possible for an already marginal academic environment such as theological education to confront the deeply entrenched power dynamics of academic practice? To speak very personally, can an institution such as mine, an interdisciplinary graduate program straddling the "divide" between theology and religious practice, afford to critique the very ground upon which it is struggling to assert that it has a right to exist? In a context in which specific areas of focus (worship, homiletics, education, pastoral care, for instance) are already criticized for being "too practical" and not "analytical" enough, wouldn't it be dangerous to threaten our standing even further by taking on such a conflicted issue?

It is in answering this question that a nonfoundational understanding of knowledge becomes most useful. In fact, it is in considering the ramifications of a question even formulated in this way that it is possible to begin to catch a glimpse of white supremacy in action. As Frankenberg illuminates, within a context structured by white supremacy, there is no language for paying attention to it. It feels awkward, for example, every time I write "white supremacy" in the context of my own theological work. That phrase has always conjured up images of the KKK, "skinheads," and other "Others" from whom I can distinguish myself. The languages, the practices, the methods and pedagogies of graduate theological education in the contexts I'm familiar with have been the "norm," the standard to which I can (as a white person) reasonably aspire. "Mastering" a discipline is considered a reasonable outcome; in fact, it is the achievement for which the credential of a "master's degree" is awarded. Yet what has it meant to be a "master" in past U.S. history? Do we (that is, white people) ever hear the past echoes of that word in celebrations in which such degrees are awarded? Let alone question the implicit assumptions of a "master of divinity" degree?

What are the underlying assumptions of a knowledge community that scorns "practice" and privileges "analysis"? In fact, what are the definitions of "practice" and "analysis" implied here? Most often "practice" refers to the embodied experiences of "Others," while "analysis" refers to the languages, experiences, and tools deemed useful by "Us"—that is, by white, middle-class, male, classically trained academics.

I am painting the picture in stark colors to enflesh Frankenberg's observation that "whiteness, as a set of normative cultural practices, is visible most clearly to those it definitively excludes and those to whom it does violence. Those who are securely housed within its borders usually do not examine it."[12] Thus, we white people don't question what it is that is making us shy away from putting dismantling racism at the heart of our work. Accepting the assumption that if we (that is, white people) "hew" to the straight and narrow we can flourish is itself indicative of conferred dominance, because there are many people for whom no matter what they did, their very presence is questioned. There is no "straight and narrow" in a context that denies existence from the outset.

The answer to the larger question posed above—whether it is possible to ask these questions in an academic environment that is already marginalized—has to be "yes." Not only is it possible, but it is vital, inescapable, crucial. It may even be our existence on the margins of graduate education that is the precondition to allowing such questions to emerge. In order to be able to ask them, let alone think through and act through responses to them, white people must make the epistemological shift away from foundational knowledge and into the framework of an epistemology that is conscious of how socially constructed any kind of knowledge is.

By deconstructing the omnipotent authority of an Enlightenment "subject" whose disembodied, universal eye/I could author knowledge that refused to recognize its thoroughgoing racism, these epistemologies give us new space within which to problematize knowing, within which to recognize not only the partial nature of our knowledge, but the oppressive ways in which it structures our lives. This is the same space in which I assert that theological education must take mediated digital cultures seriously.

There are many differing ways in which feminists deconstruct/reconstruct epistemology. Hankinson Nelson's description of "epistemological community" is one such framework that is very useful. Hankinson Nelson uses "epistemological community" to describe a way of viewing evidence that "construes evidence as communal," that "accepts coherence (and with it explanatory power) as a measure of reasonableness," and that "holds that communities, not individuals, are the primary loci of knowledge."[13] In this framework, an epistemological community discerns "what can be known" as well as the specific criteria for distinguishing between "truth and error." Yet in the broader framework that grounds an assertion of "epistemological community," there is a recognition of the partiality of any knowledge claim alongside an equal recognition that "beliefs and knowledge claims have consequences."[14] These are claims that are deeply embedded in any number of theological communities as well, whether one speaks of the ways in which discernment operates amongst a particular religious congregation or of "foundational theology," to use Francis Schüssler Fiorenza's term.[15]

Earlier in this chapter I suggested that there were many "knowledge communities" to which I am drawn. Each of these could be described as an epistemological community. The dilemma I face in finding ways to translate amongst these communities is that their ways of knowing may be in direct conflict with each other. I could respond to these conflicts in several ways: I could deny that they exist by rooting myself in those communities that construe knowledge similarly and eschewing the rest; I could move back and forth between them using the appropriate language in each and being only partly myself at any one time; or I could try to develop a new language, a "border community," that could translate among them and articulate a different understanding of "knowing." Here is a key adaptive challenge, central to the descriptions of theological education I raised in the first chapter of this book.

U.S. culture is thoroughly shaped by a "knowledge community," an "epistemological community," that I am labeling "white supremacy." It is a discourse, a language, marked more by its invisibility to white people than its presence. But absence, as the French philosophers tell us, is as remarkable as presence. The dominating discourse of white supremacy plays a crucial role in shaping the experience of everyone who lives in the United States and beyond. As a white person I can exist within it by denying it, a position comfortably supported by hegemonic apparatuses. I could attempt to be aware of it in contexts where it is obvious—primarily those where white folk are not in control, are in a "minority" position—and thus live in schizophrenia (a point well made by Terry).[16] Or I could attempt to make its language visible, confront its practices, and collaborate on new languages.

Many people have argued that racism is mitigated by digital technologies—not only do they "not know I'm a dog!" but no one "has" to make her or his race obvious. What this argument misses, however, is the underlying, deep, systemic presence of white supremacy that my argument has been tracing. As Nakamura notes:

> The study of racial cybertypes brings together the cultural layer and the computer layer; that is to say, cybertyping is the process by which computer/human interfaces, the dynamics and economics of access, and the means by which users are able to express themselves online interacts with the "cultural layer" or ideologies regarding race that they bring with them into cyberspace.[17]

I believe that white theological educators in the Christian tradition, if we are to be fully authentic and responsive to the Christian faith we espouse, must be at the leading edge of creating a "border community," of seeking a translation that allows us to affirm the call we feel, the gospel we believe in, by deconstructing white supremacy, by constantly, continually, and consistently critiquing our own practices, assumptions, and languages. Sustained contact with communities that do not benefit from the language of white supremacy is crucial in this journey. The Web provides an enormous opportunity to enter into such contact—to "make accessible" to people a variety of epistemological communities. But it also holds the risk of reifying stereotypes from other settings in this emerging culture, creating "cybertypes."

I can't be strong enough in my assertion of this statement: there is no real way to dismantle racism without learning about its effects on people whom it seeks to denigrate, deny, destroy. Yet white supremacy, an institution that uses racism as its means of effective power, is an institution created by white people in support of white dominance. Therefore it is up to white people to dismantle it, and much of that work we need to do amidst ourselves. It is not the responsibility of people of color to "teach" us how not to be racist. Whenever a person does reach out to us to do so—I am reminded here of close friends who have shared their pain with me, or the courageous writing of women like Audre Lorde, bell hooks, Lisa Nakamura—we need to value that gift in all of its preciousness and accept it with great humility.

Will the border language(s) we create have to be utterly relativist? Will it be possible to learn/create/enjoin a language that shapes a knowledge community that is both actively antiracist and yet also affirming of the global relatedness, the universality that is so often claimed for Christian knowing? This is not a question that I can answer. A notion of "epistemological community" suggests that within the dominant paradigms white people currently inhabit, such universality makes little sense. Yet the Christian community has been affirming for centuries that it carries a truth that exists for all peoples in all times. Historically that faith has been a resource both for oppression and for resistance to oppression. The search for a universal language is not the one to which I am called right now. As a white person living in the United States, I have benefited from the assumption of such a language and the powers and practices used to enforce it. Instead, I must stand on its borders, working to deconstruct such power and authority and having faith that Christian global relationship can and will continue.

LEARNING TO DISMANTLE RACISM

What do these reflections mean for the practice of theological education right now? What consequences and opportunities exist for white graduate students, faculty, and academic institutions coming to an awareness of these issues, particularly in digital cultures? We can begin by acknowledging our complicity in this system. Rather than arguing back and forth over who is racist, we (that is, white people) need to acknowledge that we are implicated in white supremacy. I am racist. I benefit from racism. Coming to that recognition, far from absolving me, in fact necessitates active conversion. Reconciliation requires active engagement in unlearning racism.

Internalized dominance, precisely because of its internalization, is difficult to recognize, let alone uproot. The work of antiracist educators points to some of the steps necessary in doing this work. The first and most important aspect that these educators share is their commitment to understanding racism as a practice created by, and used in the support of, white supremacy, with all that that term implies in the practices of power. A second crucial component these educators share is a recognition of the difficulty white people have of seeing themselves as white. As I noted earlier in this chapter, this inability is directly linked to racism's insidious practices of power: "whiteness, as a set of normative cultural practices, is visible most clearly to those it definitively excludes and those to whom it does violence. Those who are securely housed within its borders usually do not examine it."[18] Yet it is precisely the ways in which racism defines whiteness that make it crucial for white folk to understand its effect on our identities. By not scrutinizing how we are socially constructed as white, how our identities are formed and deformed by the institutionalized practices of racism, we cannot experience ourselves as fully authentic human beings.

By the same token, the possibility of growing into that kind of authentic experience makes fighting racism a journey that is directly in our own self-interest. Terry makes this point well when he writes that

> human beings are resources to each other. Racism clouds our capacity to make accurate judgements. Thus Whites end up being stupid, inept, socially incompetent, and fearful. We cannot be with and for ourselves or each other if we do not know who we are and what we are about. Thus racism forces us into inauthenticity and denies humanity to ourselves and to those we touch.[19]

It is important for me to clarify here that while I believe that fighting racism is in white people's best interests, it is also clear that we benefit from racism. So confronting it will inevitably require us to engage in the hard work of refusing the material and cultural benefits that derive from it. The way in which racism is intimately entangled in our identities as white folk makes the problem of unlearning it one of having to transform a central aspect of our identities, and having to do so while remaining enmeshed in institutions that themselves form and deform us through institutionalized racism.

Far from being shy about the ways in which our graduate programs in religious education engage "practice," we need to celebrate and learn from this engagement. We need to be very consciously and consistently active in ensuring that that practice reflects the breadth and depth of varied religious communities. In my own most immediate and personal context, there is not one "Catholic knowledge community." The advent of digital technologies makes the opportunity to work *with* other diverse Catholic communities more possible within theological education. Within a Christian context—within a wider interreligious context—we (white people) need to be ever vigilant about ensuring the widest possible conversations that take place on the most even ground. This will require a deeply spiritual practice of humility for white people. As in so many other contemplative practices, we need to learn to let go of control, we need to open ourselves up to the unsettling of the frameworks from which we've benefited. We (white people) need to place ourselves on uneven ground, on lower ground, on uncertain ground. We might even begin to have some empathy for such a position as we struggle to use digital technologies in which our students are already fluent.

To put it in very concrete terms: how in my daily life am I formed as "white" in a raced society? How do the images, the music, the rituals of liturgy, contribute to solidifying this identity, or resisting it? How does my engagement online shape my identity? Here the work of religious educators concerned with formation and catechesis may be helpful if it can turn their ideas and tools into a focus on how we are socialized into racism. Here the work of asynchronous online educators is also illustrative, because they are finding creative ways to engage students in holistic, embodied reflection that questions the "taken for granted" assumptions of learning.

How do the demands of our graduate programs form or resist white supremacy? If we can begin to uncover how the formation occurs, we can provide alternatives. I've already noted the extent to which actively dismantling racism is not a valued component of the knowledge I need to acquire for my professional credentials, but it is crucial for my ability to function authentically and nonoppressively in the communities to which I am drawn and to which I will return. I can work to ensure that every course I teach, every paper I write, contributes to this effort in some way. How does the theologian I'm reading engage racism? Is it a nonissue? Why? What consequences does such silence create? Does the developmental theory I'm tracing account for the differing demands placed upon white people and people of color? Are "higher" stages of development more readily achievable by white people? Warning bells should ring. Does the history I'm tracing engage the material differences present between white people and people of color? When I'm planning liturgy do the images present in the texts and songs I choose support white supremacy, or unlearning racism? How diverse are the faculty I interact with? How diverse are the graduate students? How diverse are the staff? In what ways do the technologies we're using privilege certain kinds of access? Who is involved in making policy choices about teaching and learning, about digital technologies? These are only a few of the questions that occur to me, and I am certain that there are far more that I have not yet begun to recognize.

Again: why is this important? I could clearly make a theological argument, inviting us to ponder the wisdom of Galatians 3:28, or invoking the claim that "we are many parts, but we are all one Body." But even in narrower terms, the richer the diversity, the deeper the opportunity to learn and to know.

As I have from the beginning of this chapter, I am arguing that racism is a central determining characteristic of life in the United States. If we are to confront it adequately, we white people need to confront our own formation as "white" in a raced society. What are the practices and pedagogies necessary for dismantling racism? I mentioned earlier some of the shared characteristics that antiracist educators bring to the task. I'd like to conclude by lifting up a process that is particularly appropriate in this context.

Katie Cannon has developed a process called "the dance of redemption" that provides a way to approach a specific problem while yet engaging diverse resources and ensuring connections to community(ies) (see fig. 6.1).[20] This process has seven steps, envisioned as cyclical and ongoing. There is no

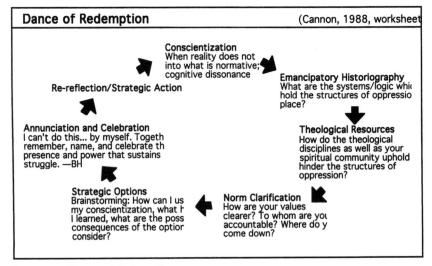

Figure 6.1   Dance of Redemption

way to "finish" this process; one can only move through it with various questions and from various standpoints. Yet it is explicitly designed to provide ways to assess and celebrate progress, thus nourishing one's continued journey in the "dance."

The "dance of redemption" strikes me as a rich resource for many reasons, not the least of which is that it provides clear and direct evidence of the need to understand how one is enmeshed in various communities. In addition, the process recommends that conscientization does not proceed directly to action, but is only the beginning point from which a more sustained and comprehensive analysis proceeds. It is also a process that very clearly embodies a belief that no one can undertake the work of building transformative community by themselves. Doing such work is by definition a collective struggle, even while one's own work has individual components to it.

Cannon's dance requires the development of strategic action as well as celebration of the process in which we are engaged. Perhaps even more crucially, by making annunciation/celebration a core part of her process, she provides a way to celebrate each step of the journey, to recognize movement and growth, and to remain aware of the progress being made in what is a very long, very difficult journey. Hers is a powerful metaphor for the relational journey that is transformative learning.

It is also a process white people need to engage if we are ever to be capable of authentic religious education of ourselves, let alone anyone else. It is time that graduate programs, graduate students, and faculty take this dance seriously, particularly as we enter new teaching environments such as cyberspace. As Nakamura notes, "the internet is a place where race happens"—and it can also be a place in which we begin to deconstruct and reconstruct our social relationships.

On more than one occasion I have found that engaging issues of racism directly can be managed constructively in online discussions. Discussions that were caught up in emotion in a typical classroom, making it difficult for some students to participate, grew more analytical when the discussion was continued online. It has also been relatively easier for me develop courses that engage a host of oppressive dynamics in online formats—not because the format necessarily lends itself to the discussion any more than a typical classroom does, but rather because some of the institutions where I have taught were so eager to have classes put into online distributed formats that I was able to negotiate for courses that engaged such content more directly and systematically than so-called core courses typically did. This room for experimentation and exploration is precious and likely to be short-lived. Yet that is all the more reason for theological educators to move into it as fully and substantively as we can. We must, at the same time, retain the humility and self-criticism that allow us to learn. To return to the passage from Paul's second letter to the Corinthians that I reflected upon in the first chapter of this book:

> We are afflicted in every way, but not crushed; perplexed, but not driven to despair; persecuted, but not forsaken; struck down, but not destroyed; always carrying in the body the death of Jesus, so that the life of Jesus may also be made visible in our bodies. For while we live, we are always being given up to death for Jesus' sake, so that the life of Jesus may be made visible in our mortal flesh.[21]

As I have argued throughout this book, and in particular in this chapter, our flesh is made visible in so many more ways than simply when we are in each other's physical presence. We are truly embodied people, and using digital technologies to communicate does not erase that embodiment. Given the sheer reach and increasing ubiquity of digital technologies, our embodiment requires ever more thoughtful reflection.

FOR FURTHER REFLECTION

Books

Adams, Maurianne, Lee Anne Bell, and Pat Griffin, eds. *Teaching for Diversity and Social Justice*. New York: Routledge, 1997.

Conley, Dalton. *Being Black, Living in the Red: Race, Wealth, and Social Policy in America*. Berkeley and Los Angeles: University of California Press, 1999.

Katz, Judith. *White Awareness: Handbook for Anti-racism Training*. Norman: University of Oklahoma Press, 1978.

Lipsitz, George. *The Possessive Investment in Whiteness*. Philadelphia: Temple University Press, 1998.

Volf, Miroslav. *Exclusion and Embrace: A Theological Exploration of Identity, Otherness, and Reconciliation*. Nashville: Abingdon Press, 1996.

Media

American History X. DVD. Directed by Tony Kaye. New Line Home Video, 1998.

Changing Lanes. DVD. Directed by Roger Michell. Paramount Home Video, 2002.

Race: The Power of an Illusion. Executive producer Larry Adelman. California Newsreel, 2003. More information is available on a PBS companion Web site, http://www.pbs.org/race/000_General/000_00-Home.htm (accessed on May 13, 2004).

NOTES

1. See chap. 3 for a discussion of the "null" curriculum.

2. Some of the best information available on the "digital divide" can be found at DigitalDivide.org, a site supported by the Benton Foundation (http://www.digitaldividenetwork.org/content/sections/index.cfm) (accessed on May 13, 2004). The Pew Project on the Internet and American Life (http://www.pewinternet.org/index.asp) (accessed on May 13, 2004) also hosts a number of important studies, including several that deal with digital issues and communities of faith in the United States.

3. Kenneth Bruffee, *Collaborative Learning: Higher Education, Interdependence, and the Authority of Knowledge* (Baltimore: Johns Hopkins University Press, 1993), 222.

4. Peggy McIntosh, "White Privilege: Unpacking the Invisible Knapsack," *Peace and Freedom* (July/August 1989), 10.

5. McIntosh, "Unpacking," 11.

6. Ruth Frankenberg, *White Women, Race Matters: The Social Construction of Whiteness* (Minneapolis: University of Minnesota Press, 1993), 14.

7. Frankenberg, *White Women*, 14.

8. Frankenberg, *White Women*, 14.

9. Robyn Grinter, "Multicultural or Anti-racist Education? The Need to Choose," in *Cultural Diversity and the Schools: Education for Cultural Diversity, Convergence, and Divergence*, ed. J. Lynch, C. Modgil, and S. Modgil (London: Falmer Press, 1992), 101–2.

10. Lisa Nakamura, *Cybertypes: Race, Ethnicity, and Identity on the Internet* (New York: Routledge, 2002), 21.

11. Nakamura, *Cybertypes*, 73.

12. Frankenberg, *White Women*, 228–29.

13. Lynn Hankinson Nelson, "Epistemological Communities," in *Feminist Epistemologies*, ed. Linda Alcoff and Elizabeth Potter (New York: Routledge, 1993), 131.

14. Hankinson Nelson, "Epistemological Communities," 151.

15. Francis Schüssler Fiorenza, *Foundational Theology: Jesus and the Church* (New York: Crossroad, 1984).

16. Robert Terry, "The Negative Impact on White Values," in *Impacts of Racism on White Americans,* ed. Benjamin Bowser and Raymond Hunt (Beverly Hills, CA: Sage Publications, 1981).

17. Nakamura, *Cybertypes*, 3.

18. Frankenberg, *White Women*, 228–29.

19. Terry, "Negative Impact," 149.

20. Katie Cannon, "The Dance of Redemption" (Lecture given at a Grailville Workshop done jointly with Elizabeth Schüssler Fiorenza, December 1–3, 1989, Grailville, Loveland, OH). The image is taken from the worksheet that was handed out as part of Cannon's presentation.

21. 2 Cor. 4:8–10, NRSV.

Chapter Seven

Freeing Culture: Copyright and Teaching in Digital Media

The problems that cyberspace reveals are not problems with cyberspace. They are real-space problems that cyberspace shows us we must now resolve.

— Lawrence Lessig, *Code and Other Laws of Cyberspace*

The essays in this book seek primarily to invite you to engage your practice as a teacher in theological education, particularly in emerging learning contexts opened up through digital technologies. In doing so I need to touch briefly on several of the intellectual property debates flourishing in this context. There are at least three worth considering: who owns (and to some extent controls) the materials we create and use in digital environments, who owns (and in what way do they control) previously published work in print as it moves into digital formats, and who owns the data, the materials with which we need to work as we seek to engage digital cultures in our teaching?

The first issue—who owns what we create in these contexts—is a hotly contested issue at many institutions. Unlike typical scholarly practice, where what we create as we teach and what we write in our research is assumed to "belong" to us (copyright for work written while a faculty member, for instance, almost always belongs to the faculty member), several institutions have argued that course resources—indeed, entire courses—developed in digital formats are "work for hire" and thus belong to the institution that employs the faculty member. Many scholars are not even aware of such rules until they attempt to take their course resources with them when they move to a different institution and are unable to do so.[1] To be fair to institutional concerns, providing digital equipment is often a heavy capital expense, and these institutions seek to hold on to their investment. On the other hand, the entire scholarly enterprise is built around open access and peer review of research, which militates strongly against such ownership.

At a minimum, it is important for faculty members to be clear about the rules and policies governing the development of such resources at our institutions. In my own context, several of us have consistently argued that digital resources of all kinds—including the bulk of any online courses we develop—ought to be freely accessible and in the open on the Internet. This argument has at least two advantages. First, it makes our research and learning as widely available as possible, and second, because no "profit" can be directly tied to its Web publication, our institution is much less interested in controlling its ownership. Some have argued that doing this weakens our entire structure, since we are essentially "giving away" that to which our students pay tuition to get access. Like MIT, however, we believe that the strength of our teaching and learning really resides in the relational interactions between teacher and students, and these—particularly course conversations and one-on-one advising—are kept behind password protected firewalls and in other enclosed spaces.[2] There are clearly theological arguments embedded here, to which I will return in a moment.

The second issue—who owns materials originally published in print and now made available in digital format—resides primarily in the question of who controls publication of such material. In the few short years that I have been a faculty member, I have watched the copyright agreements I am asked to sign in various contexts shift dramatically. Those of us who are still junior in the process of tenure eligibility—and to be fair, many of the scholars who are creating digital resources and working in digital contexts are often newer to academe—are often faced with draconian copyright agreements that create difficult dilemmas: do I sign away all rights—including the digital ones—to this piece of work I've struggled to produce, or do I refuse to sign such an agreement and lose access to credentialed publication? In a few cases scholars have been successful in keeping at least limited digital rights—the ability to publish their own work on their own Web site, for instance, or to be alerted to ways in which their print work might be transported into digital formats— but even these limited rights are often denied.

The question of such ownership is not simply a dilemma for early career scholars, but also for entire fields of study. Many prestigious journals own decades' worth of still-relevant materials, but refuse to make those materials available in digital formats at a reasonable price. Debate rages in scholarly library circles over the role periodical publishers are playing in controlling access to scholarly output. Here the argument that an institution owns the work produced by its faculty comes back with more constructive resonance. If institutions own their faculty's work, then it does not make sense for institutions to give away all rights to such materials to journal publishers simply in exchange for publication, particularly when the institution must then pay exorbitant fees to gain access to the journals in which the work is published.

The final dilemma I noted at the beginning of this chapter is the question of who controls access to the materials we need to work with if we are to take seriously the popular cultural contexts we inhabit. If I want to show clips from various television shows in my class, for instance, is this permissible? What if I want to do the same thing in a wholly online course, where doing so requires that I make the clips available in digital format via the Web—and thus accessible to a potentially endless number of downloads? What if I then want to publish a book that contains a CD-ROM of clips from movies, popular songs, and so on that are illustrations and evidence for my scholarly argument? On more than one occasion in my own career, I have been stymied by institutional answers to these questions that privilege the avoiding of potential risk of litigation over access to materials for the scholarly process. What constitutes "fair use" of digital materials is a densely complicated and hotly contested question, but even where it is clear that a particular use of materials qualifies within the "fair use" provisions, fear of litigation can often still prevent their use.[3]

My own personal example of this "chilling effect" comes from a chapter I wrote recently for a book in which I wanted to set the scene for my argument by quoting a bit of lyric from a popular U2 song. The chapter I was writing centered on supporting the development of religious identity in media culture. Using a piece of popular culture (such as a partial lyric from a song) in the essay was germane, pertinent, and appropriate in that context. Yet the publisher of the book, fearing litigation and not having a reasonably easy way to clear rights, refused to allow me to keep the lyric in my chapter. This is a very small example—it did not even involve moving images or sound media—but it hit close to home for me. The dilemmas surrounding film, particularly film resources such as "extras" made available only in macrovision-protected DVD format, are even thornier. To even "capture" an excerpt from a DVD to use in another format can potentially require the use of software that breaks the encryption on a DVD, thus exposing one to potential criminal prosecution under the DMCA (Digital Millennium Copyright Act), which made it a crime not only to pirate digital materials but even to own the equipment (including code) that would make such copying possible.[4]

All three of these issues—control of the creation of digital resources, control of the transfer of work first created in print format to digital formats, and control of the raw materials necessary for scholarly inquiry in digital cultures—rely on copyright and other regulatory frameworks created long before digital technologies ever emerged. Lawrence Lessig is arguably the most eloquent and

informed commentator currently writing on these issues. His trilogy of books—
Code, The Future of Ideas, and *Free Culture*—makes several important arguments about the architecture of the Internet and the consequences of that architecture for our cultural well-being. At heart, his argument is a sophisticated
reclamation of legal theory surrounding the original development of copyright
in the United States.

Countering the popular perception of copyright—that it exists to promote
private, individual ownership of intellectual property for the financial benefit
of the creator of such property—Lessig argues that, historically and legally,
copyright was developed as a mechanism to ensure that there was a balance
between providing an incentive for artistic creation (a reason for an artist to
struggle for a long time to create a song, for instance, might be to earn something from selling it) and making such work available to a wide audience as
part of supporting the common good (which is enriched by having access to
a cultural commons in which creativity and intellectual engagement flourish).
For a long period of U.S. history, copyright was strictly limited. It was per-
fectly legal, for example, to take a work written in one language and translate
it as directly as possible into another language without copyright permission
to do so. It was also permissible to take a story and turn it into a play or con-
vert it into some other genre without seeking permission. Initially copyright
was held to endure for the short period of fourteen years.[5]

By 2004, however, all of that has changed. Copyright is now something
that accrues instantly to anything set down in tangible form. My son's
scrawled drawing on a disposable restaurant placemat, for instance, is copyrighted without needing to do anything to suggest that he wants that protection for it. The legal term of copyright is currently set at the life of the
author—*plus* seventy years—providing enormous control over any tangible
creative work. In addition, even if one were to seek legal permission to use
previously copyrighted material in new work, because the protection accrues
instantly and without any requirement of registration, it is often nearly impossible to contact a particular creator or to sort through who owns what part
of a particular creation.[6] Popular argument suggests that such protections are
necessary for the support of the artist, but in reality most of the current law
surrounding such media benefits the corporations that distribute creative
work rather than the individuals who create it. This is in large part because of
the litigious nature of the questions, which means that only those who have
the time and financial resources to litigate for answers can do so.

Why does this matter to theological educators? Why should we care about
copyright legislation or how digital materials are distributed? I can think of
many reasons, but at a minimum, if we're going to make good pedagogical
choices —"think through culture" in all four ways noted in earlier chapters of

this book—we need access to such materials. Why should we care? Because the scholarly and educational enterprise is about production and distribution of ideas, of building on the old to create the new amidst a cultural commons—and the legal context we are in, in the United States is rapidly collapsing that cultural commons.

We live in a visual, mass mediated culture—people make sense of their lives in religious terms in the middle of this cultural database—we *must* be engaging this database, and we can't do so without engaging these materials. Yet the very materials we need to work with are increasingly being put out of our reach through copyright, patent, and other forms of law and regulation. Indeed, it may surprise you to learn that while hundreds of years of newspapers are easily accessible in many libraries and museums through the mediation of microform materials, television shows and films are not. First, there are not the same kinds of regulations in place that require newspapers and books to be deposited at the Library of Congress, and in addition, many of the media in which these materials are created (video, film, and so on) deteriorate over time. Given the ubiquity of digital tools and the rapidly decreasing price of large hard-disk storage space, you might believe that this is a small dilemma, easily repaired by digitizing such materials and making them available via the Internet or some other repository. You would be wrong, but not because the technology is not available. No, the technology is easily available—and there are insightful people who would love to make such materials available for research and archiving—but the copyright regulations are such that seeking permission to make such materials available is next to impossible.[7]

Christians believe that God continues to reveal Godself in our midst, not simply at one point in history, but throughout history. I have tried to argue in earlier sections of this book that one of the crucial resources that theological educators need to draw on is digital popular culture and that, indeed, the primary reason to engage digital technology in theological classrooms is precisely to have access to the cultural constructions that people are engaged in creating. God continues to reveal Godself in the midst of digital cultures, and if we do not engage these cultures, we miss elements of that revelation. Religious meaning-making, religious experience, is taking place in mass mediated culture, and that meaning-making shapes even those contexts where digital cultures are least apparent (in traditional worship, for instance). Religious meaning-making is being not only produced and circulated in media cultures but also contested there, and in ways that are critically important to the world at-large. Scholars and teachers of religion (both those in religious studies and those in seminaries) need to have access to the conceptual and analytical tools necessary to study popular culture as well as to basic primary source materials. Yet these materials are increasingly being held in private hands, and even basic fair use access is being so restricted by factors beyond legislation (such as litigation) as to make "fair use" a meaningless concept. In the world beyond seminaries and theological education, it has been librarians who have been the group most able to engage this challenge, but graduate theological educators (and our librarians) have rarely taken up these issues. We have a vital stake in them and important resources to bring to meeting the challenge.

It is not just as educators that we must personally care about the ways in which our course materials are held and distributed, but as theologians reflecting on the larger world we inhabit. And it is not just the materials themselves but also the kinds of code in which they are held that we ought to be conscious of. I wrote in chapter 4 about the differences in learning experiences shaped by particular kinds of software (the primary example I used was of e-mail listservers compared to Web-based bulletin boards). I wrote in chapter 6 about the ways in which even such a socially constructed and embodied characteristic as "race" can be inscribed in our learning environments. Here I need both to recall those arguments and to extend them further to ask us to question the kinds of technology policy choices we make in our theological environments.

Right now there is another battle being waged in the United States—and also globally. I'm not sure this battle has a catchy name associated with it, and it's not always easy to identify the "sides" in the conflict. But the battle I am referring to is intimately bound up in the challenge of studying mass mediated popular culture. That is the battle over who has access to and control over digital materials. More and more of mass mediated popular culture exists in digital form. Television, radio, film, and mass-market magazines are just a few examples of digitally produced media. And that doesn't even touch on the Internet, the Web, and the rest of the born-digital information ecosystem.

There have been a number of battles fought in this war quite recently, and those of us who care about relational knowing, those of us who care about having multiple and diverse voices present at the table, those of us who believe that we are fundamentally relational creatures, are losing these battles. Consider recent federal legislation. The Digital Millennium Copyright Act is perhaps one of the most disastrous of these laws, but the Patriot Act followed it up by making it more likely that the federal government would enter private library records without the patrons even knowing the records had been accessed.[8]

In 2003 the Federal Communications Commission ruled that media consolidation could continue unabated. And in 2003 the Supreme Court ruled against Eric Eldred's attempt to reopen the border of the public domain (cf. http://eldred.cc/). All of these laws and decisions can be contested, but the reality is that we're losing ground in the process. Even the changes enacted to expand fair use to digital materials don't really impact the deeper problems that attend a medium that can be licensed rather than simply protected by copyright.

We've lost these skirmishes, and the next battleground moves deeper into our territory, as people like Senator Orrin Hatch propose hardware "solutions" that would enable media industry owners to reach down through electronic lines and "bomb" computers that appear to have illegal materials on them.[9] As Lawrence Lessig points out so eloquently in his book *Code and Other Laws of Cyberspace,* while many people believe that the Internet's architecture prevents hijacking by private, commercial concerns and thus is "safe" in some way, others are very effectively moving in to change its architecture on the deep level of infrastructure, coding out decentralization and coding in the prerogatives of big industries.

Decisions such as whether to regulate broadband Internet access with a "cable" set of rules (in which case pipeline owners typically control content moving over such access) or with a "phone system" set of rules (in which case pipelines owners are explicitly prohibited from controlling content) are being reached largely outside of public conversation and debate. I would suspect that in most theological schools, at least if they're like mine, people don't even know that these debates are occurring, let alone that they could have enormously destructive consequences for religious meaning-making.

We, as sinful human beings, can never fully know where and how God may be revealed to us. But for just a moment, imagine that God might be revealing Godself in the middle of mass mediated popular culture. And imagine that the next generation of theologians will be those who interpret these cultural productions, who "read the signs of the times," so to speak. How will they do so if they cannot even bring such materials into churches, into seminary classrooms, if they cannot playfully improvise with the various data to be found in these vast cultural databases? Lessig quotes John Seely Brown: "We're building an architecture that unleashes 60% of the brain [and] a legal system that closes down that part of the brain."[10]

There has been tremendous industry outcry over the huge amount of music downloading that has taken place over the Internet. People decry the immorality of youth and bemoan the perceived lack of ethics that has young people sharing a whole range of cultural materials in digital format with each other, blithely ignoring the commercial prerogatives of such wholesale sharing. But how often have we wondered whether in fact such sharing might be an essential element of human narrative creation? And how often have theologians pondered the ethics at the heart of such sharing? Perhaps theologians, after such study, would still find much to condemn. I certainly believe that artists are entitled to recognition and appropriate payment for their work.

But right now most of the payment for such cultural production doesn't go to the artists but instead to the industries of distribution. As Lessig noted recently, "The RIAA is the Recording Industry Association of America. It is not the Recording Industry and Artists Association of America. It says its concern is artists. That's true, in just the sense that a cattle rancher is concerned about its cattle."[11] Fewer and fewer corporations own more and more of that distribution capacity. This is not healthy. It is not healthy for a democracy, and it is certainly not healthy for a community of faith.

Rather than supporting a system, an infrastructure, that seeks to build unity through imposed sameness, we need to support a system that invites unity through diversity. And doing so means getting involved in the very real decisions that are being made right now about how we will engage meaning-making, how we will know, in the cultures we are creating together.

I don't think that it is a coincidence that a film like *The Matrix* centers on an exploration of what is real and climaxes as its main character is "resurrected" by the kiss of a woman named Trinity. Nor do I think it's a coincidence that a generation of people confronted with the evident hypocrisy and structural deceptions of various churches should turn to a "secular" film to finally find evidence that the Christ story has narrative resonance for them. As Margaret Miles notes, "the representation and examination of values and moral commitments does not presently occur most pointedly in churches, synagogues, or mosques, but before the eyes of 'congregations' in movie theaters. North Americans—even those with religious affiliations—now gather about cinema and television screens rather than in churches to ponder the moral quandaries of American life."[12]

Are we going to leave such pondering to float only within the frames created by mass media content producers? Are we going to continue to rely only upon the data their search engine makes accessible to us? Or are we going to learn how to improvise, both *with* the data available there and beyond it with *data* that we produce ourselves?

Recently Jed Horovitz produced an evocative commentary on one of the more lucrative battles that big media companies are currently waging against cultural improvisers. Titled *Willful Infringement*, this DVD provides multiple examples of ways in which culture is *always* about making new things out of old ones. Disney would not be in the position it currently holds, for instance, able to successfully lobby to extend copyright protection so far into the future, had such protection existed when it began its efforts in animation. Religious meaning-making is no different. As Mary Boys writes, religious education is "the making accessible of the traditions of the religious community and the making manifest of the intrinsic connection between traditions and transformation."[13] And as Terrence Tilley points out, "*tradita* alone do not carry the tradition. . . . the greater the difference between the context in which the *traditor* learned the tradition and the context in which the tradition is transmitted, the greater the possibility that a shift in *tradita* may be necessary to communicate the tradition. Paradoxically, fidelity to a tradition may sometimes involve extensive reworking of the *tradita*."[14]

If we are serious, both about giving people access to our traditions and the deep understanding of how those traditions are always in a process of transformation, then we will need to learn to improvise, we will need to learn to "shift the 'tradita'" sufficiently. And that process will require that we work with the cultural databases around us. Doing so will mean that we need to play with digital media, and most pertinently for this argument, with things from within mass mediated popular culture contexts: to "rip, mix, burn," as Apple puts it.

This kind of improvisation is so crucial that I want to lift up a few additional reasons in support of it from within a Christian theological framework. I'm sure there are also many reasons that would be compelling within other frames, but as those are not the primary context in which I work, I'll leave those arguments to others.

I have three from within Christian theology that I would lift up in particular.

First, as I noted earlier, we believe in a God who is within Godself most essentially *relational*. We believe in a God who is Creator, Redeemer, and Sanctifier. A God who knows us through relationship, and thus whom we know through relationship. If our knowing is so thoroughly relational, and if that relationality is produced, circulated, negotiated, and contested within cultural contexts pervaded by popular culture, then it is constitutive of "ourselves in relation" to engage that culture.[15]

Following from that, then, one of the central heartbeats of Christianity—for both better and worse—has been our sending out into the world. "Go therefore and make disciples of all nations," writes the author of the Gospel of Matthew, in chapter 28. This is an imperative for mission. Yet one of the deep consequences of a relational epistemology is both a clear recognition of the ways in which we have lived out that mission quite destructively in some contexts and a renewed challenge to try again. In other words, we are drawn into mission not because we seek to impose our beliefs on others but because we know, deep in our souls, that we can only really *know* what we believe with as wide and deep a matrix of knowers as possible. Indeed, our sacred narrative invites us to move outward in the deep humility of a pilgrim on a journey of transformation. We are invited to "try out" our beliefs with other people in other contexts, not to *prove* our interpretation, but in fact to *risk* it. Mass mediated popular cultures are just some among the many in which we seek to learn, a point that returns to the issues I raised in the first chapter of this book.

Third, there are powerful issues of distributive and social justice being contested in the middle of the mass media right now. I have mentioned some of the more obvious in terms of access to forms of knowing, but there are many others—issues concerning the ever widening digital divide, issues involving the sustained promotion of policies of consumption that make the United States the "20 percent of the world's population who uses 67 percent of the world's resources and generates 75 percent of its pollution," and so on.[16] Many of these issues are "masked" in some ways because the cultural databases we draw on are often narrow and limited. It is not simply that religious communities need to improvise with popular culture to engage positive forms of revelation occurring there, but also that we need to be trenchant critics of the narrowness of the databases, we need to have sufficient imagination to see what is beyond the confines of the dominant frame. What lies outside Google?

WHAT CAN THEOLOGICAL EDUCATORS DO ABOUT THIS?

So what can theological educators do about any of this? Like any difficult challenge, there are numerous possible responses, and no one institution will be able to handle all of them. Maybe there's only one thing on this list that you can manage to implement. Small steps are important! I hope that this list might also spark you to ideas that haven't occurred to me. That is, after all, part of the benefit of relational approaches to knowing.

Prayer and Worship

To begin with, one easy step would be to bring these issues into community prayer. There is probably no more central way into a community's heart than through its prayer life. Similarly, if you preach in worship at your institution, consider studying the texts you might be engaging to see what insight they could challenge you with in relation to these issues. One of the reasons our communities are not aware of these issues is because those of us in pastoral leadership who have such awareness are not weaving the concerns into our daily practices and into our corporate worship life. Indeed, rather than simply accepting that the copyright practices of the larger culture need drive the cultural productions within our communities, we ought to be actively and creatively promoting alternatives. Religious communities are among the very few institutions left in the United States that are not permeated by narratives of profit seeking and profit maximization. If there is going to be any space to nurture alternative narratives, we ought to be at the forefront of it. Throughout this book I have included in the resources for further reflection at the end of each chapter several such resources that are available on the Web, or in CD-ROM or DVD formats.

Simple Steps

There are many other small ways to encourage your institution, your department, even individual colleagues to support these initiatives. The "take back the public domain" petition (http://www.petitiononline.com/eldred/petition .html) is one such example. It doesn't take much effort to sign a petition, but it's a place to start conversation. Another such opportunity is to ask your institution to sign on to the Budapest Open Access Initiative (http://www.soros .org/openaccess/). The Association of College and Research Libraries has done so, as have several universities around the globe. Very few, if any, theological institutions have taken this step.

Creative Commons Licensing

Another opportunity available to theological educators is to support the deliberate and intentional limitation of copyright on the materials we create for use in our classes. Lessig and others have developed legal language and an easy mechanism for retaining limited kinds of copyright: copyright that allows others to reproduce your materials in educational settings with proper attribution, for instance, or a copyright permission that permits others to freely modify and distribute your work. These licenses are available free at the Creativecommons.org Web site and are remarkably easy to use. Given the parameters of academic work more generally—peer review, open access, and so on—it is logical both to want to put our materials out to share and be improved upon and also to want to do so in a way that protects them from unauthorized use commercially. Creative Commons licensing provides a mechanism within our current copyright regimes to positively give people access to the work we produce while allowing us to retain certain kinds of rights. Such licensing, combined with the ease of distribution promoted by digital technologies, suggests yet another opportunity: open source collaborative development.

Open Source Development

Seminaries in particular, but religious and theological studies programs more generally, ought to take a strong open source stance. "Open source" is a term that originally applied to software that was developed in a particularly open way.[17] Since then it has come to be applied to a range of processes that invite a vast array of volunteers into the development and distribution of a particular product.[18]

We can make clear policy choices within our institutions to support open source solutions. Some of these may already be evolving, given the economic challenges we face with the ever increasing price for licensing proprietary software. But I think that beyond the immediate "bottom line" calculations, we need to be ready to support open source work even if it's difficult, even if it costs more in the short term, even if we find ourselves becoming less efficient in some ways. It may be less efficient, but if the process of development involves a wider range of people and creates tools and other resources that are easily circulated, then it will be worth it. We can use Linux-based servers, for instance, instead of Microsoft servers. We can deliberately develop computer resources that begin and remain open source.

Open source ideas also push far beyond the information technology arena. We can advocate for and implement policies that keep course resources developed at our institutions free and in the open, in publicly accessible places. MIT's Open Knowledge Initiative is perhaps the most famous example of this kind of commitment. Obviously there ought to be some exceptions to making course content public—the conversations that occur within a class between teacher and students, for instance—but aside from such exceptions, our theological reasons *to do so* ought to override even economic ones not to. The Disseminary (http://www.disseminary.org/), born through the wise innovation of A. K. M. Adams at Seabury-Western, is one example of an institution trying to do this within the theological context. Why aren't more theological institutions leading the way? Or at least following?

Further, we can move beyond just course content and support scholarly and research resources kept publicly and in the open. Here again the Disseminary provides a nice example. But why aren't more of our core peer-reviewed journals moving to this model? The Rowe.com fiasco of 2003 was particularly painful for the business of academic serials publishing. Maybe it's time to take a leap beyond that model completely. It is highly problematic to me that the bulk of religious resources available on the Web have little or no provenance from established religious institutions. We are dragging our feet entirely too much in this arena, and we ought to be out front rather than stumbling along behind. Let's build the theological DSpace (http://www.dspace.org/).

Chris Locke, Doc Searls, and David Weinberger listed very persuasively in the Cluetrain Manifesto (http://www.cluetrain.com/) a set of ninety-five theses in relation to the burgeoning Internet community. Their first thesis is that "markets are conversations," and their second is that "markets consist of human beings." There is a huge conversation going on out there that we in religious institutions ought to be a part of. Now is the time to take some risks and believe enough in what we're doing to move beyond the old distribution models and into the new—particularly when those models support human relationality. We could begin to do so even with our older journals by finding creative ways to make existing content accessible in richly annotated formats. The Association of Theological Libraries has one initiative that is digitizing and making available theological journals. But full text availability, while it is helpful to scholars and others who know how to access such research, is not yet as immediately useful as something like what the *Teachers College Record* has done with its site.

The *Teachers College Record* has organized a rich assortment of its previous journal content around specific areas of interest that open up its content to more casual browsers of the Web. The content of the articles hasn't been changed, it's still profoundly scholarly and rigorous, but the organizational links, the pathways by which people find the content, have multiplied and in the process created a much more dense and hypertext-woven fabric. The site includes a mechanism allowing for community comment, a kind of open forum in which people who come to a particular content area can post questions or responses. Similar sites might be developed for other journals within theological education, in the process bringing substantial content to the Web.

It would be a very interesting and instructive exercise—perhaps even sufficient for a master's-level thesis—to consider systematically a journal's entire output, its entire range of issues over the years, and then to develop categories, content areas, by which to organize themes and recurring ideas. Even research that has clearly been superseded by more recent findings might remain interesting as historical context. Such a project would provide rich data for the graduate student working on it and would also have a tangible and useful outcome if it led to ease of access on the Web.

Most institutions of graduate theological education are more directly connected to actual living, breathing communities of practice than much of academe is. We ought to be able to lead the way here, our convictions ought to be drawing us outward rather than creating yet more barriers behind which we keep our evermore irrelevant knowledge. Religious knowing is *not* irrelevant, but institutionalized religious knowing, kept rigidly in linear, instrumental frameworks of "experts" and "amateurs," does become so.

What might it look like if even just one faculty, student, or staff member of each of our institutions maintained a weblog linked to the Disseminary, for instance? What might it look like if basic media education and technological literacy were a part of all of our faculty, staff, and student development efforts? The number of theological schools, particularly in the mainline Christian denominations, that support varieties of media engagement has actually gone down over the last two decades rather than increased. We may be adding digital capabilities to our institutions, but we are having a hard time using those capabilities to explore media cultures, let alone provide living bridges between the work we do within academe and the actual practice of the communities of faith we serve and study.

The possibilities are nearly endless, but here is an example of what such development might look like in the context of my own field, particularly if focused on strengthening both the academic enterprise and the local church community.

Open Source Curriculum Development

Imagine a Web site, for instance, where any church, any community of faith, could publish the things it had created to support religious learning and religious practice. This Web site would be freely accessible to the public, so that anyone could post resources—curriculum materials, Bible studies, worship notes, and so on—and anyone could download them. The key would be that anyone publishing materials through the site would need to agree—in the posting—that the resources would be there under a Creative Commons copyright agreement to stay free and accessible.[19] Contributors would be able to work out separate agreements with print publishers only as long as the original electronic publications remained free and open.

So, begin by imagining a Web space in which people from all over the world could publish the resources they've developed locally and others could download and use these resources—perhaps modifying and reposting them back to the Web site, further contextualized for use in specific settings.

Now, imagine that this Web site has two additional features—a powerful search engine that allows people to search in multiple ways amongst the materials and a powerful and flexible review system that allows anyone who chooses to, to add their own evaluation of the materials.

Finally, imagine groups of people all over the world—religious education professors at seminaries, for instance, and local groups of religious educators in a specific denomination—who regularly go to this site and engage in evaluation of published materials there. Individual readers of the site could develop their own ratings of the critics and begin to use both keyword search criteria as well as their critics' favorites to quickly and easily find materials that they can use in their own context.

There are already some Web sites available that provide some of this functionality in other contexts. HollywoodJesus.com (http://www.hollywood jesus.com/), for instance, is a public space for discussing popular films and their use within religious settings. The Workshop Rotation (http://www

.rotation.org/) model for Sunday school curricula is a space in which people are experimenting with curriculum development together. Perhaps the Internet Sacred Texts Archive (http://www.sacred-texts.com/index.htm) or the Disseminary (http://www.disseminary.org/) are additional illustrative examples. From the larger digital world, Slashdot (http://slashdot.org/) is a Web site where people regularly post information and then rank each other's postings and engage in community discussions of various aspects of such postings. Amazon.com is a powerful database of available materials for purchase, but it also has a collection of reviewers who regularly review materials.

What might be the obstacles? Some would claim that such a site would need an editorial board to review material before it is posted. Certainly there are analogues to such sites. Merlot (http://www.merlot.org/Home.po), for instance, recruits and trains editors to oversee the materials being placed on its site. Such a site serves the specific and useful purpose of placing "already vetted" materials in the public domain. Yet it does not contribute much to developing the editorial and assessment capabilities of the communities it serves, instead holding those tasks closer to its administrative structure. An open source development project could have as one of its primary goals supporting the creation and nurture of precisely those capabilities—assessment and editorial contextualization.

Such a site could be wide open in such a way that anything could be posted.[20] The process of publication on the site would require authors to identify themselves (that is, no anonymous publication would be allowed) and to accept a Creative Commons license for their work. The key editorial work would come from individuals and communities who regularly go to the site either to find materials—and later post their experiences with them—or to evaluate materials (as in students from higher education classes, for whom teachers would make it an assignment to practice their evaluation skills on materials from the site).

The editorial function would thus grow organically with the users of the site and at the same time would be nurturing the discernment abilities of communities of faith. As particular evaluators become recognized as providing wise editorial remarks, their own authority within the community would grow. In the past many churches simply looked to their denominational publishers for authoritative content, assuming that whatever the publisher sold must be doctrinally sound and educationally appropriate. Setting aside for the moment a judgment about whether or not that process ever worked well, we can say that it does not work at the *current* moment.

Communities of faith are simply too diverse, and situated in too many different contexts, for print publishers to be able to produce such materials in a timely, cost-effective, theologically sound, and pedagogically appropriate way. There are, of course, some exceptions. And there are certainly materials that work best in print—full-color reference books, for instance. Still, publishing companies are finding it very difficult to use the old print models for developing and selling content in the current era (e.g., see the Cluetrain Manifesto for a longer discussion of the ways in which the new technologies are reshaping our modes of production).[21]

Further, communities of faith simply cannot afford to leave such judgments to people not organically linked to them, no matter how theologically astute and biblically informed they might be. We must, within communities of faith, learn what our criteria for evaluation are and how to apply them. We cannot leave all such judgments to others, particularly if doing so means that we avoid learning how to do this kind of discernment. This challenge becomes particularly pressing at the graduate level in seminaries. The students in our Christian education classes, for instance, not only need to know how to *support* learning, they also need to know how to *design* effective learning. And to do *that*, they need to have finely honed evaluative abilities. They can no longer rely, as some once did, on simply "grabbing off the shelf" the denominational publisher's Sunday school curriculum. Instead, they need to assess what kinds of materials best serve their particular contexts.

The Web site envisioned in this thought experiment could provide a catalyst for the development of such abilities. Students in seminaries and other graduate theological contexts regularly write Bible studies, learning units, and other such materials as assignments in their courses. I have noticed that when they are required to make those units available to actual communities, students are much more rigorous in their design. At the same time, communities of faith are hungry for materials that respond to specific needs "at the moment." The Web site envisioned in this thought experiment could create a space that faculty and students from around the country could participate in and learn from.

Accessibility

One final note that that last sentence urges me to make: if we are concerned about making our materials, our scholarship, available in ways that become widely accessible, then we ought to take "accessibility" particularly seriously. Many of our institutions have invested large capital resources in making buildings physically accessible but have not done the same with our electronic resources. There are a host of ways to ensure that Web sites, for instance, are easily accessible to people who are blind, but how often do our institutions actually keep this goal in front of us?

These are just a few ideas. I hope that you will have more. I pray that together we can find many more. I fear that if we do not, we risk more than simply institutional irrelevance. We risk turning away from active engagement with our living, breathing, incarnate, and ever revealing God.

FOR FURTHER REFLECTION

Films

Willful Infringement. DVD. Directed by Greg Hittelman, Fiat Lucre, 2003. More information available at http://www.willfulinfringement.com/ (accessed on May 13, 2004).

Web Sites

Bobby Worldwide. http://bobby.watchfire.com/bobby/html/en/index.jsp (accessed on May 13, 2004).
Creative Commons. http://creativecommons.org/ (accessed on May 13, 2004).
DSpace. Web site. http://libraries.mit.edu/dspace-mit/ (accessed on May 13, 2004).
The Disseminary. http://disseminary.org/ (accessed on May 13, 2004).
Electronic Frontier Foundation. http://www.eff.org/ (accessed on May 13, 2004).
Illegal Art. http://www.illegal-art.org/ (accessed on May 13, 2004).
The Internet Archive. http://www.archive.org/ (accessed on May 13, 2004).
The Open Courseware Initiative. http://ocw.mit.edu/index.html (accessed on May 13, 2004).
Stanford Copyright and Fair Use Center. http://fairuse.stanford.edu/ (accessed on May 13, 2004).
The Web Accessibility Initiative. http://www.w3.org/WAI/ (accessed on May 13, 2004).

NOTES

1. It is always worth asking, for instance, what is involved in "porting" your materials from one online course format to another. The technical tools to do so often remain in the hands of IT administrators who answer to institutional authorities rather than faculty members.

2. MIT has initiated two major projects in the last decade that help to make their commitment to keeping their resources out in the open and publicly accessible. The OpenCourseWare Initiative (http://ocw.mit.edu/index.html) makes course resources freely accessible, and DSpace (http://libraries.mit.edu/dspace-mit/) provides a digital repository for materials created at MIT (accessed on May 13, 2004).

3. This is a point Lawrence Lessig makes abundantly clear in several of his publications. "Fair use" is an argument for allowing copyrighted materials to be used in educational and research settings without seeking permission from the copyright owners. Generally it involves four kinds of questions about the use the work might be put to: (1) What is the character of the use? (2) What is the nature of the work to be used? (3) Will the use decrease the value of the work? (4) Does the user believe the use is fair? There are numerous resources listed at the end of this chapter for further reflection on what constitutes "fair use."

4. The Stanford University Library Web site that covers issues of copyright and fair use has a particularly good collection of links about the DMCA (http://fairuse .stanford.edu/primary_materials/legislation/dmca.html) (accessed on May 13, 2004).

5. Lawrence Lessig, *The Future of Ideas* (New York: Random House, 2001), 107.

6. This is an argument Lawrence Lessig makes particularly well in *Free Culture: How Big Media Uses Technology and the Law to Lock Down Culture and Control Creativity* (New York: Penguin Books, 2004).

7. Brewster Kahle's efforts to support the Internet Archive are a good example of a resource that has encountered numerous obstacles due to copyright law. You can learn more about the Internet Archive at: http://www.archive.org/ (accessed on May 13, 2004).

8. More information on the DMCA can be found at: http://fairuse.stanford.edu/ primary_materials/legislation/dmca.html (accessed on May 13, 2004). More information on the Patriot Act can be found at the American Libraries Association site, http:// www.ala.org/ala/oif/ifissues/usapatriotactlibrary.htm (accessed on May 13, 2004).

9. As the Berkman Center for Internet & Society at Harvard Law School reported recently in their newsletter (the *Filter,* 5.9), Senator Hatch was quoted as saying: "'There's no excuse for anybody violating copyright laws. [. . .] If we can find some ways to [stop piracy] short of destroying their machines, I'd like to know what it is. But if that's the only way, then I'm all for destroying their machines.'—Senator Orrin Hatch (R-Utah), arguing a recent hearing in Washington that a legitimate legislative remedy for copyright infringement on the Internet would be to destroy infringers' computers."

10. Lessig quoting John Seely Brown, in *Free Culture,* 47.

11. Lawrence Lessig, as quoted by the *Filter,* 5.9.

12. Margaret Miles, *Seeing and Believing: Religion and Values in the Movies* (Boston: Beacon Press, 1996), 25.

13. Mary Boys, *Educating in Faith: Maps and Visions* (San Francisco: Harper and Row, 1989), 193.

14. Terrence Tilley, *Inventing Catholic Tradition* (Maryknoll, NY: Orbis Books, 2000), 29.

15. Many contemporary theologians are working at integrating new work in cultural studies with theology. One of the more interesting collections, from which this idea is drawn, is Delwin Brown, Sheila Davaney, and Kathryn Tanner, eds., *Converging on Culture: Theologians in Dialogue with Cultural Analysis and Criticism* (New York: Oxford University Press, 2001), 5.

16. Barbara Kingsolver, *Small Wonder* (New York: HarperCollins, 2002), 113.

17. For the strict definition of "open source" in relation to software, see the Web site: http://www.opensource.org/docs/definition.php (accessed on May 13, 2004).

18. One of the original essays that pushed the definition's implications beyond software was Eric Raymond's "The Cathedral and the Bazaar," since included in a book by that name, but still available on the Internet at: http://www.catb.org/~esr/writings/cathedral-bazaar/cathedral-bazaar/ (accessed on May 13, 2004).

19. The Creative Commons license agreements allow for a variety of choices. More information can be found at: http://creativecommons.org/ (accessed on May 13, 2004).

20. There would clearly need to be some limits, likely identified over time by the community itself (no inflammatory language, no obvious commercial activity, etc.). Other such Web sites provide models in this regard (e.g., http://slashdot.org/faq/).

21. The Cluetrain Manifesto was written by Chris Locke, Doc Searls, and David Weinberger and is available on the Web at http://www.cluetrain.com (accessed on May 13, 2004).

Chapter Eight

Seeing, Hearing, Creating: Exercises That Are "Low Tech" but That Engage Media Cultures

One of the persistent concerns often raised when attempting to integrate digital technologies into graduate theological education is that it is so expensive. This concern assumes that doing such integration requires institutions to purchase large amounts of equipment. While I believe that there are many advantages that come from having equipment "in house," there are also many ways to engage digital cultures with very "low-tech" tools. In this final chapter I will explore three separate learning exercises that all have at their core learning goals related to integrating theological reflection and digital cultures. They are also exercises that seek to engage students on all three levels—cognitive, affective, and psychomotor—and that are flexible and open to participation in many different settings. Finally, they are exercises that encourage exploration of digital cultures and meaning-making without using digital technology.

THE RULE OF THREES

This is an exercise that takes at least an hour and a half but can go much longer depending on how many people you have.[1] The first half of the exercise takes approximately thirty-five minutes. To determine the remainder of the time required, allow at least five minutes of processing for each small-group poster; and then, finally, you will need at least twenty minutes for "meta"-stage processing.

You will need a variety of basic materials:

- A stack of recent pop culture magazines that you don't mind cutting up. I usually use several issues of magazines like *Time* or *Newsweek*, *Entertainment Weekly* or *People*, *Good Housekeeping* or *More*, *Glamour* or *Self*,

Rolling Stone or *Spin,* and so on. You can often get discarded copies of such magazines from people in and around your institution (friends, staff people, students, etc.). For this exercise to work well, however, try to find only mass-market, supermarket-stand-type magazines.

- Enough scissors and glue for every participant.
- At least one sheet of heavier-weight paper or tagboard that is about 8.5 × 11 inches in size or larger for each small group.
- A music player of some sort and some quiet instrumental background music.
- An evocative question that has explicit theological elements and admits of diverse responses. Choosing the question to which you seek answers is probably the most difficult part of this exercise. You will need a question that is open enough to elicit several responses but also focused enough to allow the groups to share ideas from their experience. Questions that have worked well in my courses in the past include: What does it mean to be Catholic? What is redemption? Who is God? and so on.

Divide your participants into smaller groups of about three to five people. Explain that each group is going to construct a poster that will offer an answer to the same question. Each group will have thirty minutes to construct its poster and may use no more than three images and three words cut out from the magazines provided—hence the "rule of threes." Post the question somewhere where it will be highly visible, turn on some quiet music, and have the groups gather their materials and begin working.

Give the groups a five-minute warning as you draw close to the thirty-minute mark, and then call time at thirty minutes. Ask the students to rejoin the large group and bring their posters to a central place in the room. Open a discussion on each poster in turn. Begin by explaining to students that for the initial discussion of a poster, anyone who contributed to the construction of that particular poster is to refrain from speaking and simply listen to what their colleagues have to say about it. Ask the rest of the students to voice what they believe the poster "says." What is the answer being offered to the shared question?

Once you've gotten the basic responses out into the open, deepen the reflection by asking students to focus on the specific construction of the poster. Was there anything problematic about the images that were chosen? (Are all the images of people white, for instance? Are they all male? Are there extraneous elements of a particular image that contest the meaning the poster offers? and so on.) Once the reflections begin to end, invite the small group that constructed the poster to reflect out loud on what they heard. Did their colleagues "get" the message they were trying to send? Were there any surprises in what they heard?

Repeat this process for all of the posters in turn.

Once you've completed discussing each poster individually, ask the group to reflect on the process itself: What did they learn from this exercise? What was most difficult? What surprised them? and so on. By this point most students have begun to figure out that there is something interesting about the creativity that is spurred by specific constraints—time constraints, material constraints, format constraints, and so on. They are also usually beginning to sense the complexity involved in making meaning with images. No poster ever conveys precisely what its creators intend, and most people improvise more meaning from a particular set of images than the creators of the images can imagine. Further, taking images from one context and placing them in another often radically shifts the meaning made with them.

As a final topic of discussion, ask the students to reflect on the process of looking for images that convey specific theological meaning amidst the multiplicity of images offered up via popular culture. How large was the pool of possible images? Were there images they were seeking and couldn't find? How much interpretative ability do they think people need to function well in media culture? The exercise is often best concluded by reminding students that this is the kind of process behind much creative production in mass mediated popular culture—working very fast, in small groups of people, from a limited database of possibilities, and within specific constraints. (And even when that is said and done, as ad executives are fond of saying about commercials, "We know that 50 percent of our commercials will be successful, we just can't predict which 50 percent!")

This exercise clearly has multiple layers and evokes a variety of intelligences. Students who can draw on spatial and visual forms of intelligence can contribute much more in this kind of exercise than is usually the case in purely text-driven encounters. Students who are deeply steeped in theological themes will be able to bring them to the table and will be challenged to embed those themes in the nonlinear format of image. The discussion is shaped in such a way as to invite initial reflection on the experience a student is having (whether in looking at a specific poster or in reflecting on the process more generally), and then to move from there to reasoning that is more analytical (what images contribute to particular meanings? what images are problematic? etc.) and synthetic (how can we reflect theologically across multiple media?). Individual student responses are invited, but the group process also suggests that individual experience alone is not as rich a source of learning as is a carefully framed group process.

All of these elements are critical for the learning goals I have within my religious education courses. At the same time—almost as a bonus—the exercise helps students to reflect upon theological imagination in media culture, and to do so without once using a piece of digital technology (although using multiple images created by digital technologies). The point is to reflect upon digital cultures and the process of creative production in digital culture, to reflect upon theological imagination and its expression in mass mediated contexts, and so invite students into more active engagement with their own meaning-making.

MUSIC AS AN ELEMENT OF SONIC ENVIRONMENT

Another exercise that invites students to reflect upon the meaning they make with an element of mass mediated popular culture is the "sonic environment" exercise.[2] This exercise takes about an hour to accomplish and can be used in a group as small as five or as large as your room can accommodate.

For this exercise you will need a variety of music CDs or MP3s and a music system with good speakers that can replay the music well. Choose three groups of music, with four pieces of music in each group. Each piece of music should be instrumental, although since you will only be sharing thirty seconds of it with listeners, you can easily choose pieces that begin instrumentally even if they later include words. I will have more to suggest about how to choose music, but first let me outline the exercise.

Begin by dividing your large group into smaller groups of no more than twenty-five people (if you have fewer than that to begin with, simply remain in one group). Explain to students that they will need a piece of paper and a writing instrument and that you will be asking them to listen to some short excerpts of music and to respond to those excerpts briefly in writing. Make certain that you stress that this is an exercise that has no "right" or "wrong" answers and that students may keep their responses private if they so choose. Explain that the music will be grouped into three sections and that after each section there will be some group discussion time.

For the first section, ask the students to listen to each piece of music as it is played and then write down the *color* it evokes for them. They should note it quickly, not try to analyze their response, and prepare for the next piece of music. Their list at the end of the four pieces might look like this: 1. green, 2. blue, 3. purple, 4. black, and so on. After you've played all four pieces, go around the group and ask each student to say what color they wrote down for each piece of music. Remind them that there are no "right" or "wrong" answers and that they are free to pass and not share their response. Don't belabor the process too much, but at the end allow general feelings to be expressed. Often there is general amazement and surprise, for instance, at how many of the responses fall into the same color families.

For the second section of the exercise (the next group of four pieces), ask the students to write down an *adjective* describing what they are feeling as they listen to each piece of music. Again, stress that this should be a quick, "off the top of the head" response that they should not analyze. As before, once all four pieces have been heard and noted, go around the room for each piece and elicit the responses students wrote down. Here again, don't belabor the process, but at the end allow for general feelings to be expressed.

Finally, for the third section of the exercise, ask the students to write down a *sentence* that captures the story the music might be trying to tell. Here you will likely want to leave a slightly longer pause between pieces of music. When you've finished playing the music, again return to the group and go around the room asking for responses. This is the section of the exercise where I've most often had students pass on their turn, so it is often useful to remind them, again, that it's fine to choose not to share if they would prefer not to.

After completing the process for all three sections, return to the large group (if you have divided previously), and ask students to reflect upon what, if anything, they've learned in this process. Responses often cluster around surprise at how much different responses have in common, how evocative music can be, and so on. Then ask students to consider what implications this exercise might hold for their specific contexts. Students who are musicians involved with planning liturgies, for instance, often talk about wanting an entire liturgy to have a "color" to it. Students who are planning to preach often suggest that they ought to be more attentive to planning with the church musicians for the environment in which their sermon will be embedded. Students who plan learning events will often speak of the ways in which their imagination has been expanded to think about how they incorporate music into what they are doing—not simply in terms of songs they will teach but also in terms of the music playing in the background while they work.

Finally, I have often found it fruitful to ask students to reflect upon what they think I might have intended to accomplish by using this kind of exercise. It is almost impossible to predict the answers I receive to that question, but it gives me an appropriate opening to talk about the ways in which embodied knowing shapes our learning, even if we do not consciously attend to it.

Clearly one of the crucial elements in the success of this exercise is choosing appropriate music. I strive to find music that is quite diverse, usually drawing on a variety of genres. Movie soundtracks have been particularly fruitful resources for me, because they frequently paint quite deliberate "colors" using only instruments or voices with no discernible lyrics (although I try to stay away from movie soundtracks that are particularly famous). I also usually include at least one piece of Native American flute music. Given the contexts in which I teach, heavy metal Christian music is fun to use because it tends to subvert expectations. When the exercise is over, students often ask what the pieces were, and when they discover that the harsh, driven music they put deep colors and emotions to (red and black often come up there, or angry and frustrated) is from a Christian group, they tend to pause and reflect on whether knowing something about the producer of the music alters their reception of it.

At the heart of this learning exercise is an invitation to students to consider the multiple ways in which they engage various kinds of music and the layers of meaning that attend to sonic environments, whether they are paying attention to them or not. In designing learning environments—as in planning liturgy—it is important to attend to the implicit and null curricula as much as to the explicit curriculum. Sonic environment is one element that far more often falls into the implicit or null elements of curriculum design.

Given the ease of use of digital sound tools, particularly the compression format MP3, which has made the sharing of music so easy, more and more people have the technical capabilities necessary to attend to their sonic environments. So-called mix tapes (cassettes of different songs that people record and share) have been a part of the pop culture scene since audiocassettes were invented, but the availability of tools to make and share music mixes in digital format has expanded the practice exponentially. In addition, more and more of the most popular television shows are embedding music marketing into their format. You can watch *Joan of Arcadia,* for instance, and learn from the credits who the "featured artists" were. You can then go to the Web and buy such music from a site like iTunes. Such practices encourage a high degree of attention to sound, and to the shaping of one's context through sound, as well as to the promotion of meaning-making stretched over many more contexts than the original television show. More traditional church contexts need to attend to this process, not to duplicate the commercialization of music, but rather to respect the depth of experience and interpretive ability people bring to their music experiences.

Hymns that once conveyed important theological meaning in their lyrics may not be conveying such meaning to listeners who are embedded in music that has freer rhythms and more flowing melodies. The "sound" of such hymns in some contexts conveys regimentation and imposed order rather than freedom granted by God. The solution to such a dilemma is not to throw out traditional hymns and bring in only contemporary pop music—as some church folk have proposed—but rather to be more hospitable to the multiple meanings people are making with various kinds of music and more respectful of the role sonic environment plays in shaping such meaning. We can ask each other, across multiple contexts, how does our music *mean?* What are the stories embedded in the songs we love? For some those stories are carried by particular lyrics, but for most of us the stories attach rather more to what we were doing when we first heard a song, who was holding us in their arms when first we sang that song, and so on. A learning exercise like this one invites us into appreciation for the complexity of such meaning-making.

VIDEO REALITY GAME

The final learning exercise I'll describe requires rather more technology to work, although here again it is technology that is usually readily available even in church basements: a TV and a VCR.[3] This video exercise usually requires from an hour to an hour and a half to complete and can be used in a group as small as ten people, although it works very well in very large groups, too, as long as everyone can see the TV monitor and hear what is going on.

For this exercise you will need seven roughly three-minute-long video clips from broadcast television (more about that in a moment), a blackboard or whiteboard or newsprint to write on in front of the group, and a piece of paper and a writing instrument for each participant.

Begin by drawing a horizontal line on the chalkboard (or whiteboard, etc.), with the word "real" on the right-hand end of the line. Make the line as long as you can, and ask students to replicate the drawing on their own piece of paper. Explain that this is a reality spectrum, that you are going to show them various short video clips, and that you are going to ask them to place each clip somewhere on that spectrum. Already at this point in the explanation I am usually interrupted by students who want to know what word to place on the opposite end and what "real" means. I tell them that part of what we'll be exploring in this exercise are responses to those questions. In the meantime, they should simply try to engage the exercise as it comes. Here, as in the last two exercises I've described, there are no "right" or "wrong" answers, and students should always feel free to keep their responses private. Next, explain that you will be inviting a person to volunteer prior to each clip and that once the particular clip has been shown, that volunteer will come up front and place the clip on the large spectrum in front. Volunteers may also share why they've placed the clip there, if they choose to do so.

Go ahead and show the clips in the order you've chosen in advance. Remember to invite volunteers *prior to* showing the clip (so they don't know what they're about to see), and then remember to give them time to come up front and mark the clip on the spectrum. Most people will immediately recognize at least the genre of the clip you're using, if not the precise show from which it's drawn. It is useful to remind the group from time to time that they should be thinking about their own spectrum, not assuming that theirs should echo the one up front.

Once you've shown the clips, the first question to ask is usually "Does anyone's spectrum match the one up front?" In all of the years I've been doing this exercise, I've never once had anyone whose drawing did. A point to draw out here is that everyone approaches media from their own location and will make meaning with it in highly personal ways. One way to explore such meaning-making is to invite students to talk about the criteria they used in placing clips. This is usually a very fruitful question, and people do not hesitate to brainstorm about it. Write the criteria up on the board in front of the room, and do your best to be encouraging. If you don't understand a particular response, you can always invite the student to elaborate on the idea by explaining how he or she used it to place clips.

If students' responses do not include reflecting on the particular production elements of the videos, I will usually add those as criteria as well, pointing out that different genres carry meaning in different ways (soap operas have low production values and are produced on a budget, whereas prime-time dramas have higher budgets, etc.; new media are framed in certain ways, and Saturday morning cartoons in others). Once all of the criteria have been written down, go through the list and see what kinds of themes emerge. In general this exercise usually elicits a lot of criteria based in some way on students' experiences—"It feels true to me," "I've been in similar situations," "It didn't feel real, I felt manipulated"—and so on. I generally have to push to get at other possible criteria that could emerge, among them elements of genre, production, and so on. This exercise has been at the heart of my own shift over the years to recognizing the profoundly affective ways in which people make meaning in mediated contexts. As Thomas Boomershine has noted, we tend to reason more by means of sympathetic identification than philosophical argument in our current media climate. At the same time, however, such identification must needs be stretched—particularly in an environment where only certain experiences are embedded in mediated representations.

After talking about the criteria the students are using, I then shift the discussion to the question of what is "real" and what term they had in their mind as the opposite end of the spectrum. Here the discussion can quickly become quite philosophical as students struggle to figure out what the relationship is between notions of "real" that mean "material reality" or "evidence" and notions that have more the connotation of "truth" or "absolute ground of existence." The opposite end of the spectrum might be "false," "unreal," "hyperreal," "surreal," and so on, but what qualifies under that term usually varies greatly from student to student. Is a particular clip more "real" or "true" because it has a Bible verse embedded in it? Is it more real because it "feels" more real to me or because it aligns more completely with a particular understanding of truth? Here again the conversation can go in multiple directions. I tend to work toward keeping the *questions* as open as possible, laying the groundwork for more discussion in later sections of my courses. This is not an exercise aimed at arriving at a common definition of reality, but rather one focused on problematizing the perceptions of reality that students have when they enter my class.

In my own teaching, the layer of "content" meaning I've tried to include in this exercise clusters around representations of religion and religious persons. All of the clips I use carry some element of religious representation in them, and that allows me to invite students to reflect on the "religious education" people receive within media culture before they ever walk in the door of a church or other faith community.

Here, as in the sonic environment exercise, the choice of clips you use is important. I generally use seven clips and draw them from a variety of genres. I use something from a soap opera, from a newsmagazine, from a PBS documentary, from a children's show, from a cartoon, from a prime-time drama, and I usually also include a clip that is a broadcast of a religious service. Each clip is no longer than three minutes and has to have some internal consistency. That is, the clip I use from a drama is an entire scene, the exchange from a newsmagazine is at least one question asked and answered, and so on.

I gather these clips simply from regular television viewing (a chore that has been made much easier by our purchase of a ReplayTV digital video recorder). Shows such as *The West Wing, Joan of Arcadia,* and *The Simpsons* are usually very fruitful for grabbing clips with religious representation embedded in them. Newsmagazine shows often run specials around the release of particular movies, so if there is a movie coming out with a religious theme (a much more frequent occurrence these days), then taping *20/20* or *Primetime* or *The Today Show* often yields useful materials. Evening newscasts frequently have religious stories on them on Sundays or in the days preceding major religious holidays. I have not had as much luck with soap operas, although *One Life to Live* has a recurring character who is a priest and has, at least in the past, produced some interesting and evocative story lines. VeggieTales, a popular animated children's series, is often the one exception to my rule of using only broadcast clips. The series is sold primarily via videotape and DVD and is not regularly broadcast, but it is almost always good for a brief and amusing clip and is a good example for problematizing the embedding of biblical text in video.

When I first encountered this video exercise, it was done around the representation of violence and was very effective. I think you could also implement it using the representation of gender, race, class, ethnicity, age, or any of a number of other cultural characteristics as the lens through which you choose clips. It is a remarkably flexible exercise for generating critical reflection along with enjoyable engagement. A final comment I would make about it is that I have found it a very useful evaluation tool when used at the beginning of a course. I often try it on the first day of my classes—that session when you cannot assume that students have read any of the course materials yet—and it provides a way for me to draw them into collaboration right away. I learn a lot about who in the class likes this kind of exercise and who does not, who can frame their experiences critically and who is not yet able to do so, and so on. I also learn a lot about students' attitudes toward popular culture and their familiarity (or lack thereof) with media education.

CONCLUSION

All three of these exercises provide an entry point into quite sophisticated and complex descriptions of the social construction of reality, but they do so in a way that invites participation whatever kind of meaning-making participants are most familiar with. I have used each of these exercises in a variety of different settings, with participants ranging in age from ten to eighty-eight. Clearly I have different kinds of emphases in specific classes, but overall my goal is to invite people into a deeper and more reflective stance toward the media cultures they inhabit. While there are many ways in which these exercises could use digital technologies (the music exercise could use MP3s, for instance, and the creative exercise could be based on students using digital cameras to capture images rather than cutting them out of magazines), they do not require such technologies to be effective. Instead, they can invite us into deeper engagement with the mediation of meaning using quite basic, nondigital materials.

Two of these exercises were developed in the context of media education aimed at the K–12 level. What fascinates me most about them is that they have proven equally engaging for my oldest students. There is a wealth of media education material available via the Web, and much of it can be adapted toward the goal of "real-time" theological reflection. Doing so provides multiple levels of learning: it engages students' theological "muscles," it stretches their assumptions about media cultures, it challenges their assumptions about basic pedagogy. I dare to hope that it also, as the group Jars of Clay sings, helps us to "see the art in me" and draw us outward in wonder at all that God has created amongst us.[4]

FOR FURTHER REFLECTION

California Newsreel. http://www.newsreel.org/ (accessed May 13, 2004).

The Center for Media Literacy. http://www.medialit.org/ (accessed May 13, 2004).

The Jesuit Communication Project. http://interact.uoregon.edu/medialit/JCP/index.html (accessed May 13, 2004).

The Media Education Foundation. http://www.mediaed.org/ (accessed May 13, 2004).

The Media Literacy Review. http://interact.uoregon.edu/MediaLit/mlr/home/index.html (accessed May 13, 2004).

The Media Research and Action Project. http://www.bc.edu/bc_org/avp/cas/soc/mrap/default.html (accessed May 13, 2004).

The New Media Bible. http://www.newmediabible.org/ (accessed May 13, 2004).

NOTES

1. I have adapted this exercise from one I first encountered in the Felton Media Literacy Scholars seminar taught by Professor Renee Hobbs in Boston, MA. More information on Dr. Hobbs's work is available at http://www.reneehobbs.org/ (accessed on May 13, 2004).

2. This exercise was created by Professor Fabio Pasqualetti of the Facoltá di Scienze della Comunicazione Sociale of the Salesian Pontifical University, Rome, Italy. I first experienced it during a workshop at the Mexican American Cultural Center in San Antonio, TX, in 2003.

3. This exercise is another one adapted from the work of Renee Hobbs and the Felton Media Literacy Seminar.

4. Jars of Clay, "Art in Me," from the compact disc *Jars of Clay*, Jive, 1995.

Bibliography

Adams, Maurianne, Lee Anne Bell, and Pat Griffin, eds. *Teaching for Diversity and Social Justice.* New York: Routledge, 1997.

Alexander, Hanan. *Reclaiming Goodness: Education and the Spiritual Quest.* Notre Dame, IN: University of Notre Dame Press, 2001.

Beaudoin, Thomas. *Virtual Faith: The Irreverent Spiritual Quest of Generation X.* San Francisco: Jossey-Bass, 1998.

Blood, Rebecca. *The Weblog Handbook: Practical Advice on Creating and Maintaining Your Weblog.* Cambridge, MA: Perseus Publishing, 2002.

Boys, Mary. *Educating in Faith: Maps and Visions.* San Francisco: Harper and Row, 1989.

Brookfield, Stephen. *Becoming a Critically Reflective Teacher.* San Francisco: Jossey-Bass, 1995.

———. *Discussion as a Way of Teaching: Tools and Techniques for Democratic Classrooms.* San Francisco: Jossey-Bass, 1999.

Brown, Dan. *The Da Vinci Code.* New York: Doubleday, 2003.

Brown, Delwin, Sheila Davaney, and Kathryn Tanner, eds. *Converging on Culture: Theologians in Dialogue with Cultural Analysis and Criticism.* New York: Oxford University Press, 2001.

Brueggemann, Walter. *Cadences of Home: Preaching among Exiles.* Louisville, KY: Westminster John Knox, 1997.

Bruffee, Kenneth. *Collaborative Learning: Higher Education, Interdependence, and the Authority of Knowledge.* Baltimore: Johns Hopkins University Press, 1993.

Cannon, K., K. Douglas, T. Eugene, and C. Gilkes. "Metalogues and Dialogues: Teaching the Womanist Idea." *Journal of Feminist Studies in Religion* 8, no. 2 (fall 1992).

Chopp, Rebecca. *Saving Work: Feminist Practices of Theological Education.* Louisville, KY: Westminster John Knox Press, 1995.

Conley, Dalton. *Being Black, Living in the Red: Race, Wealth, and Social Policy in America.* Berkeley and Los Angeles: University of California Press, 1999.

Daloz, Laurent A. Parks, Cheryl H. Keen, James P. Keen, and Sharon Daloz Parks. *Common Fire: Lives of Commitment in a Complex World.* Boston: Beacon Press, 1996.

Dykstra, Craig. "Evaluation as Collaborative Inquiry." *Initiatives in Religion* 2, no. 4 (fall 1993).

Eisenstein, Elizabeth. *The Printing Revolution in Early Modern Europe.* Cambridge: Cambridge University Press, 1983.

Eisner, Elliott. *The Educational Imagination.* New York: Macmillan, 1985.

Fiorenza, Francis Schüssler. *Foundational Theology: Jesus and the Church.* New York: Crossroad, 1984.

Frankenberg, Ruth. *White Women, Race Matters: The Social Construction of Whiteness.* Minneapolis: University of Minnesota Press, 1993.

Friedman, Thomas. *The Lexus and the Olive Tree.* New York: Anchor Books, 2000.

Grinter, Robyn. "Multicultural or Anti-racist Education? The Need to Choose." In *Cultural Diversity and the Schools: Education for Cultural Diversity, Convergence, and Divergence,* edited by J. Lynch, C. Modgil, and S. Modgil. London: Falmer Press, 1992.

Hankinson Nelson, Lynn. "Epistemological Communities." In *Feminist Epistemologies,* edited by Linda Alcoff and Elizabeth Potter. New York: Routledge, 1993.

Heifetz, Ronald. *Leadership without Easy Answers.* Cambridge: Harvard University Press, 1994.

hooks, bell. *Black Looks: Race and Representation.* Boston: South End Press, 1992.

———. *Talking Back: Thinking Feminist, Thinking Black.* Boston: South End Press, 1989.

———. *Yearnings: Race, Gender, and Cultural Politics.* Boston: South End Press, 1990.

hooks, bell, and Cornel West. *Breaking Bread: Insurgent Black Intellectual Life.* Boston: South End Press, 1991.

Hoover, Stewart. "The Culturalist Turn in Scholarship on Media and Religion." *Journal of Media and Religion* 1, no. 1 (2002): 25–36.

Hoover, Stewart, and Lynn Clark eds. *Practicing Religion in an Age of Media.* New York: Columbia University Press, 2002.

Hoover, Stewart, Lynn Clark, and Diane Alters. *Media, Home, and Family.* New York: Routledge, 2004.

Horton, Sarah. *The Web Teaching Guide: A Practical Guide to Creating Course Web Sites.* New Haven: Yale University Press, 2000.

Jhally, Sut, Stephen Kline, and William Leiss. *Social Communication in Advertising.* London: Routledge, 1997.

Katz, Judith. *White Awareness: Handbook for Anti-racism Training.* Norman: University of Oklahoma Press, 1978.

Kegan, Robert. *In over Our Heads: The Mental Demands of Modern Life.* Cambridge: Harvard University Press, 1994.

Kim, Amy Jo. *Community Building on the Web: Secret Strategies for Successful Online Communities.* Berkeley, CA: Peachpit Press, 2000.

Lahaye, Tim, and Jerry Jenkins. *Left Behind.* Wheaton, IL: Tyndale House Publishers, 1995.

Lessig, Lawrence. *Code and Other Laws of Cyberspace.* New York: Basic Books, 1999.

——. *Free Culture: How Big Media Uses Technology and the Law to Lock Down Culture and Control Creativity.* New York: Penguin Books, 2004.

——. *The Future of Ideas: The Fate of the Commons in a Connected World.* New York: Random House, 2001.

Lipsitz, George. *The Possessive Investment in Whiteness.* Philadelphia: Temple University Press, 1998.

McIntosh, Peggy. "White Privilege: Unpacking the Invisible Knapsack." *Peace and Freedom* (July/August 1989).

Miles, Margaret. *Seeing and Believing: Religion and Values in the Movies.* Boston: Beacon Press, 1996.

Mitchell, Jolyon, and Sofia Marriage, eds. *Mediating Religion: Conversations in Media, Religion, and Culture.* Edinburgh: T & T Clark; New York: Continuum, 2003.

Nakamura, Lisa. *Cybertypes: Race, Ethnicity, and Identity on the Internet.* New York: Routledge, 2002.

Palloff, Rena. *Building Learning Communities in Cyberspace: Effective Strategies for the Online Classroom.* San Francisco: Jossey-Bass, 1999.

Palmer, Parker. *The Courage to Teach: Exploring the Inner Landscape of a Teacher's Life.* San Francisco: Jossey-Bass, 1998.

——. *To Know As We Are Known.* San Francisco: HarperSanFrancisco, 1993.

Sample, Tex. *The Spectacle of Worship in a Wired World: Electronic Culture and the Gathered People of God.* Nashville, TN: Abingdon Press, 1998.

Seymour, Jack. "Approaches to Theological Education." Lecture, Wabash Center summer workshop, Wabash College, Crawfordsville, IN, 1999.

Shweder, Richard. *Thinking through Others: Expeditions in Cultural Psychology.* Cambridge: Harvard University Press, 1991.

Stout, Daniel, and Judith Buddenbaum, eds. *Religion and Popular Culture: Studies on the Interaction of Worldviews.* Ames: University of Iowa Press, 2001.

Tanner, Kathryn. *Theories of Culture: A New Agenda for Theology.* Minneapolis: Fortress Press, 1997.

Terry, Robert. "The Negative Impact on White Values." In *Impacts of Racism on White Americans,* edited by Benjamin Bowser and Raymond Hunt. Beverly Hills, CA: Sage Publications, 1981.

Tilley, Terrence. *Inventing Catholic Tradition.* Maryknoll, NY: Orbis Books, 2000.

Tyner, Kathleen. *Literacy in a Digital World.* Mahwah, NJ: Lawrence Earlbaum Associates, 1998.

Vella, Jane. *Learning to Listen, Learning to Teach: The Power of Dialogue in Educating Adults.* San Francisco: Jossey-Bass, 2002.

Volf, Miroslav. *Exclusion and Embrace: A Theological Exploration of Identity, Otherness, and Reconciliation.* Nashville: Abingdon Press, 1996.

Weinberger, David. *Small Pieces, Loosely Joined: A Unified Theory of the Web.* Cambridge, MA: Perseus Publishing, 2002.

Whiteley, Raewynne, and Beth Maynard. *Get Up off Your Knees: Preaching the U2 Catalog.* Cambridge, MA: Cowley Publications, 2003.

Wiggins, Grant, and Jay McTighe. *Understanding by Design.* Upper Saddle River, NJ: Merrill/Prentice Hall, 2001.

Zull, James. *The Art of Changing the Braining: Enriching Teaching by Exploring the Biology of Learning.* Sterling, VA: Stylus Publishing, 2002.

Multimedia

The Ad and the Ego. DVD. Directed by Harold Boihem. Parallax Pictures, Inc., 2004. More information available at: http://www.parallaxpictures.org/AdEgo_bin/ AE000.01b.html (accessed May 13, 2004).

A.I. DVD. Directed by Steven Spielberg. Universal Studios, 2001.

American History X. DVD. Directed by Tony Kaye. New Line Home Video, 1998.

Bend It Like Beckham. DVD. Directed by Gurinder Chadha. Twentieth Century Fox Home Video, 2003.

Beyond Borders: Ministry in the Multicultural World. CD-ROM. JMCommunications.com, 2002. This CD-ROM can be ordered online through the Mexican American Cultural Center (http://www.maccsa.org/).

Bobby Worldwide. http://bobby.watchfire.com/bobby/html/en/index.jsp (accessed on May 13, 2004).

California Newsreel. http://www.newsreel.org/ (accessed May 13, 2004).

The Center for Media Literacy. http://www.medialit.org/ (accessed May 13, 2004).

Changing Lanes. DVD. Directed by Roger Michell. Paramount Home Video, 2002.

Chapman, Tracy. "All That You Have Is Your Soul," *Crossroads.* CD. Elektra/Asylum, 1989.

Cormode, Scott. *Transforming Christian Leaders.* http://www.christianleaders.org/ (accessed on May 13, 2004).

Creative Commons. http://creativecommons.org/ (accessed on May 13, 2004).

Crow, Sheryl. "Let's Get Free," exclusive track from *iTunes,* 2003.

Dead Poets Society. DVD. Directed by Peter Weir. Touchstone Video, 1989.

Dretzin, Rachel, and Barak Goodman, producers. "The Merchants of Cool." *Frontline,* PBS, February 27, 2001. This episode is now available via the Web at: http://www.pbs.org/wgbh/pages/frontline/shows/cool/ (accessed on May 13, 2004).

DSpace. http://libraries.mit.edu/dspace-mit/ (accessed on May 13, 2004).

Dunkley, Wayne. *Share My World: A Photographic Study on Race and Perception.* http://sharemyworld.net/ (accessed on May 13, 2004).

EdTV. DVD. Directed by Ron Howard. Universal Studios, 1999.

Electronic Frontier Foundation. http://www.eff.org/ (accessed on May 13, 2004).

The Emperor's Club. DVD. Directed by Michael Hoffman. Universal Studies, 2002.

Galaxy Quest. DVD. Directed by Dean Parisot. Universal/MCA, 2003.

Nancy Griffiths, "Time of Inconvenience," *Flyer.* CD. Elektra/Asylum, 1994.

The Harry Potter Trilogy. DVD. Directed by Chris Columbus (1, 2) and Alfonso Cuarón (3). Warner Home Video, 2001–2004.

The Hurricane. DVD. Directed by Norman Jewison. Universal/MCA, 2000.

Illegal Art. http://www.illegal-art.org/ (accessed May 13, 2004).

The Internet Archive. http://www.archive.org/ (accessed May 13, 2004).

The Jesuit Communication Project. http://interact.uoregon.edu/medialit/JCP/index .html (accessed May 13, 2004).

Joan of Arcadia. Broadcast television show. Written and produced by Barbara Hall, 2004.

KAIROS, a Journal of Rhetoric, Technology, Pedagogy. (http://english.ttu.edu/kairos/ index.html).

Lavigne, Avril. "Complicated," *Let Go.* CD. Arista, 2002.

The Lord of the Rings Trilogy. DVD. Directed by Peter Jackson. New Line Home Video, 2001–2004.

Mary Hinkle's Web. http://www.luthersem.edu/mhinkle/(accessed May 13, 2004).

The Matrix. DVD. Directed by Larry Wachowski and Andy Wachowski. Warner Studios, 1999.

The Media Education Foundation. http://www.mediaed.org/ (accessed May 13, 2004).

The Media Literacy Review. http://interact.uoregon.edu/MediaLit/mlr/home/ index.html (accessed May 13, 2004).

The Media Research and Action Project. http://www.bc.edu/bc_org/avp/cas/soc/ mrap/default.html (accessed May 13, 2004).

The Mediated Spirit. CD-ROM. Written and created by Peter Horsfield, Commission for Mission, Uniting Church in Australia, 2003. More information available at: http://www.mediatedspirit.com/ (accessed on May 13, 2004).

Ministry in a Multi-cultural World: Beyond Borders. CD-ROM. Written and created by Adán Medrano, JMCommunications.com, 2003. More information available at: http://www.maccsa.org/Merchant2/merchant.mv?Screen=PROD&Store_Code=ma ccsa&Product_Code=0932545122 (accessed on May 13, 2004).

Mona Lisa Smile. DVD. Directed by Mike Newell. Columbia Tristar Home, 2003.

Mr. Holland's Opus. DVD. Directed by Stephen Herek. Hollywood Pictures, 1996.

The New Media Bible. http://www.newmediabible.org/ (accessed May 13, 2004).

The OpenCourseWare Initiative. http://ocw.mit.edu/index.html (accessed on May 13, 2004).

The Open Knowledge Initiative. http://web.mit.edu/oki/ (accessed May 13, 2004).

The Passion of the Christ. DVD. Directed by Mel Gibson. Icon Productions, 2004.

Pleasantville. DVD. Directed by Gary Ross. New Line Home Video, 1999.

Rabbit Proof Fence, DVD. Directed by Phillip Noyce. Miramax Home Entertainment, 2004.

Race: The Power of an Illusion. Executive producer Larry Adelman, California Newsreel, 2003. More information is available on a PBS companion Web site, http://www .pbs.org/race/000_General/000_00-Home.htm (accessed on May 13, 2004).

Resources for Christian Leaders. http://www.christianleaders.org/ (accessed May 13, 2004).

The Simpsons. Broadcast television show. Creator Matt Groening. Fox Television, premiered December 1989.

Stanford Copyright & Fair Use Center. http://fairuse.stanford.edu/ (accessed on May 13, 2004).

Stephen's Web on Knowledge, Learning, Community. http://www.downes.ca/ (accessed May 13, 2004).

The Truman Show. DVD. Directed by Peter Weir. Paramount Studios, 2003.

U2. *All That You Can't Leave Behind.* CD. Polygram Records, 2000.

Valparaiso Project on the Education and Formation of People in Faith. *Practicing Our Faith.* http://www.practicingourfaith.org/ and *Way to Live: Christian Practices for Teens.* http://www.waytolive.org/ (accessed on May 13, 2004).

VeggieTales. Assorted DVDs. Warner Home Video (more information available at: http://www.bigidea.com/).

The Visible Knowledge Project. http://crossroads.georgetown.edu/vkp/.

The Web Accessibility Initiative. http://www.w3.org/WAI/ (accessed on May 13, 2004).

The West Wing. Broadcast television show. Created by Aaron Sorkin. NBC Television, premiered September 1999.

Whale Rider. DVD. Directed by Niki Caro. Columbia Tristar Homevideo, 2003.

Willful Infringement. DVD. Directed by Greg Hittelman. Fiat Lucre, 2003. More information available at: http://www.willfulinfringement.com/ (accessed on May 13, 2004).

The Yale Web Style Guide. http://www.webstyleguide.com/

You've Got Mail. DVD. Directed by Nora Ephron. Universal Studios, 1998.

Index